T0190424

Beginning Photo Retouching and Restoration Using GIMP

Learn to Retouch and Restore Your Photos like a Pro

Second Edition

Phillip Whitt

Apress®

Beginning Photo Retouching and Restoration Using GIMP: Learn to Retouch and Restore Your Photos like a Pro

Phillip Whitt
Columbus, GA, USA

ISBN-13 (pbk): 978-1-4842-9264-8
https://doi.org/10.1007/978-1-4842-9265-5

ISBN-13 (electronic): 978-1-4842-9265-5

Managing Director, Apress Media LLC: Welmoed Spahr
Acquisitions Editor: Susan McDermott
Development Editor: James Markham
Coordinating Editor: Jessica Vakili

Distributed to the book trade worldwide by Springer Science+Business Media New York, 1 New York Plaza, New York, NY 10004. Phone 1-800-SPRINGER, fax (201) 348-4505, e-mail orders-ny@springer-sbm.com, or visit www.springeronline.com. Apress Media, LLC is a California LLC and the sole member (owner) is Springer Science + Business Media Finance Inc (SSBM Finance Inc). SSBM Finance Inc is a **Delaware** corporation.

For information on translations, please e-mail booktranslations@springernature.com; for reprint, paperback, or audio rights, please e-mail bookpermissions@springernature.com.

Apress titles may be purchased in bulk for academic, corporate, or promotional use. eBook versions and licenses are also available for most titles. For more information, reference our Print and eBook Bulk Sales web page at http://www.apress.com/bulk-sales.

Any source code or other supplementary material referenced by the author in this book is available to readers on the Github repository: https://github.com/Apress/Beginning-Photo-Retouching-and-Restoration-Using-GIMP. For more detailed information, please visit http://www.apress.com/source-code.

Printed on acid-free paper

This book is dedicated to my supportive family and friends.

Table of Contents

About the Author

Phillip Whitt has been a photo retouching professional since the year 2000. Over the years, Phillip has served many photographers, photo labs, and the general public, restoring and editing countless images. He also offered film-to-video transfer services for a number of years, helping people preserve precious family memories.

Prior to that, he spent the late 1980s and much of the 1990s as the advertising manager of a medium-sized hardware/home center. Much of his work required learning graphic design and working with images. This led to him eventually becoming proficient in programs such as Adobe PageMaker (which was replaced by InDesign long ago) and Photoshop.

Since 2014, Phillip has authored several books and produced several video courses for Apress Publishing pertaining to image editing.

About the Technical Reviewer

Massimo Nardone has more than 22 years of experience in security, web and mobile development, cloud, and IT architecture. His true IT passions are security and Android.

He has been programming and teaching how to program with Android, Perl, PHP, Java, VB, Python, C/C++, and MySQL for more than 20 years.

He holds a master of science degree in computing science from the University of Salerno, Italy.

He has worked as a project manager, software engineer, research engineer, chief security architect, information security manager, PCI/SCADA auditor, and senior lead IT security/cloud/SCADA architect for many years.

His technical skills include security, Android, cloud, Java, MySQL, Drupal, Cobol, Perl, web and mobile development, MongoDB, D3, Joomla, Couchbase, C/C++, WebGL, Python, Pro Rails, Django CMS, Jekyll, Scratch, etc.

He currently works as Chief Information Security Officer (CISO) for Cargotec Oyj.

He worked as visiting lecturer and supervisor for exercises at the Networking Laboratory of the Helsinki University of Technology (Aalto University). He holds four international patents (PKI, SIP, SAML, and Proxy areas).

Massimo has reviewed more than 40 IT books for different publishing companies, and he is the coauthor of *Pro Android Games* (Apress, 2015).

Acknowledgments

I'd like to acknowledge Susan McDermott and Jessica Vakili for their help and patience over the years! They are both professionals of the highest caliber.

Introduction

The Joy of Restoring Photos

When you look through your family photo album, chances are you'll notice that some of those pictures are showing their age. They might have faded, lost a great deal of color, or have stains, tears, or other forms of damage. There may be only one picture of a favorite aunt or uncle in existence, possibly in poor condition. If you have photos that are precious to you, you know how important it is to rescue and preserve them for posterity (Figure 1).

Figure 1. *A faded image rescued for future generations (Image courtesy of Bruce Bundt)*

With the advent of digital imaging software, it's now possible to perform minor miracles and revive damaged photographs that might have been considered beyond repair. In this profession, there's nothing more gratifying than the look of surprise and joy on a client's face as they gaze upon a fresh, new copy of a restored family photo for the first time. Sometimes, the client is moved to tears, which reiterates how important family photographs are. Most of us in the photo retouching and restoration profession love what we do. I personally find it very therapeutic—even when wrestling with some of the more challenging jobs that come my way. Learning these skills is a plus for photographers who want to add an extra revenue stream to their business. Genealogists can greatly benefit from knowing how to digitally resurrect images from generations past. The family archivist will have fun preserving the history of mom and dad, as well as an assortment of cousins, aunts, and uncles.

Why Photographs Are Important

Our old family photographs go largely unnoticed in our day-to-day lives. They are tucked away in aging photo albums (Figure 2), displayed in frames (often exposed to damaging light), or stored in drawers and boxes. Improper storage and exposure to UV light cause the majority of damage to photographs.

Figure 2. *Photographs kept in an aging album*

Our photographs are linked to our history. The fact is we often don't give them much thought until a milestone anniversary or birthday arrives, a loved one passes on, or other significant events occur. Throughout my career, I've had many desperate clients hire me to restore their treasured images for all of these occasions.

Preventing damage is always preferable to repairing it. Keeping photos in acid-free albums, displaying them in frames with UV-resistant glass, and keeping them out of junk drawers and boxes will go a long way toward preserving your images. It's also important to digitize them, so copies can be given to family members. Those images of our parents, grandparents, kids—even distant relatives—are part of our heritage and well worth preserving. It would be a shame if our visual family history couldn't be passed on to future generations. Fortunately, with the aid of this book, and the image-editing power of GIMP 2.10, you'll be able to rescue all of the damaged images in your family's collection, as well as those of your clients, if you choose to make a profession out of this fun and challenging activity.

GIMP: The Powerful Free Image-Editing Alternative

Years ago, there weren't many options available for full-featured photo-editing programs. Adobe Photoshop was by far the most powerful—and the most expensive. While it is still considered the leading photo-editing software, there are other options that have narrowed the gap over the years.

One of the most powerful free photo editors is the open source *GIMP* (currently in version 2.10.32).

GIMP stands for *GNU Image Manipulation Program*. The best part about it (other than being free) is that you can share it with friends and install it on multiple computers—all without fear of committing piracy or violating licensing agreements. It is issued under the terms of the GPL, which stands for *General Public License*. Photoshop is probably *the* most pirated software on earth. With GIMP, that isn't possible. The developers *encourage* you to distribute copies (and yes, it says so on their website).

Open source software such as GIMP means that the source code is openly available. Anyone with programming skills can make improvements and enhancements. There is a large community of GIMP users that contribute to its ongoing development and improvement. Over the years, GIMP has matured into a powerful tool used by many independent photographers, graphic designers, and artists who require a full-featured image editor.

In May 2013, Adobe Systems, Inc., changed to a subscription-only business model. It no longer sells physical boxed software packages or downloads with perpetual licenses. Adobe customers must pay a monthly fee to use the company's current products on a continual basis. This apparently angered many of Adobe's customers, many of whom began seeking alternatives to Adobe products, especially Photoshop. There was a dramatic increase in the download frequency of GIMP in the months that followed Adobe's decision. It would be reasonable to assume that GIMP will become more popular over time, as it keeps improving.

Although GIMP lacks some of Photoshop's features, it's still an extremely capable editor for photo retouching and restoration tasks. There are plug-ins available that can restore some of the missing features, so GIMP will become more on par with Photoshop.

To download the software and access the documentation and license, visit the official website at www.gimp.org. GIMP can be installed on Windows, Macintosh, Linux, and Unix derivatives. The website will help direct you to the correct installer (or source code) for your system.

Even though this book is a beginner's guide to photo retouching and restoration, it's not a beginner's guide to GIMP. For the benefit of those new to GIMP, Chapter 1 is an overview of some of this software's important features. It should provide beginners with enough information to follow the tutorials, but the GIMP User Manual will provide much more specific information about the software itself.

If you're a complete beginner, consider my book *Practical Glimpse* (also by Apress Publishing). Glimpse is a *fork* of GIMP (essentially meaning it has its own team of developers). With the exception of only a couple of minor things, Glimpse is identical to GIMP, so the information in the book is applicable.

The retouching and restoration techniques in this book can be replicated by other programs, such as Adobe Photoshop and Corel PaintShop Pro. However, some of the tool names and command names will differ.

If you've been eager to learn photo retouching and restoration without the high price tag that accompanies Photoshop, I encourage you to get started with GIMP 2.10. You can download the practice photos with which to follow along in each lesson.

This book will teach you how to do the following:

- Acquire the best scans and digitize oversized photos

- Improve contrast to make faded photos look their best

- Correct exposure problems

- Make color corrections in photos that have color shifts or color casts

- Colorize black-and-white photos

- Digitally clean up dust on photos (great for scanned images acquired from old 35mm slides or negatives)

- Repair images with tears, cracks, and stains

- Remove unwanted objects from photos

- Recompose portraits (add or remove people, change backgrounds, or make other changes)

- Digitally remove skin blemishes, whiten teeth, etc.

- Protect and preserve your restored images

Visualizing the Editing Steps

It will be beneficial to evaluate each photo and visualize your steps from start to finish. This may be a little challenging in the beginning, but it gets easier with practice. Outlined in the following is the progression of an image restoration that should serve as a general guide:

1. *Straighten the image*: Sometimes, the image you are working with will be tilted slightly. GIMP can easily correct this. You can see in the example (Figure 3, right-hand-side example) that the porch has been straightened. Now the edges are at an angle and will have to be cropped.

Figure 3. *The image straightened*

2. *Crop the photo*: In the next example (Figure 4), I cropped the image to the client's specifications. Photos from the 1950s were often square, and cropping eliminates the excess foreground.

3. *Make the necessary exposure and contrast adjustments*: By using a combination of layers set with the *Multiply* and *Overlay* blending modes, the photo has much better contrast and brightness (Figure 4, right-hand-side example). When editing color images, make the needed color adjustments after exposure corrections.

Figure 4. *Image cropped (left) and contrast improved (right)*

4. *Do your digital cleanup/editing*: Remove scratches, spots, blemishes, and any distracting elements. After editing, recheck the exposure and contrast. In color photos, recheck the color correction.

5. *Recheck the photo for overlooked dust, blemishes, etc.*: Give the photo a final overview, to make sure you removed all of the imperfections that might have been overlooked the first time. Once you're satisfied with the outcome, it is finished. Be sure to save a layered version of your work. (I'll explain this in greater detail in the section "Working with Layers" in Chapter 1.)

6. *Resize the image*: Resize the photo to its final output size.

7. *Sharpen the photo*: Last, sharpen the image slightly. The end result looks much better (Figure 5).

Figure 5. *Before and after comparison*

Note This process will vary somewhat, depending on the image and the editing requirements. For example, it's better to repair images with heavy damage (large cracks, tears, or missing areas, in which large patches of underlying white from missing image emulsion are visible) before making tonal and/or color corrections.

Improving with Practice

The tutorials in this book will help you learn a great deal about photo retouching and restoration. Mastering the lessons in this book will help you along the way to becoming an expert retouch or restoration artist, and with *dedicated* practice, you will become one. This is especially important if you plan to become a professional retoucher and restorer. Top-notch work that exceeds your clients' expectations will make them very happy, which can promote glowing word-of-mouth testimony leading to potential clients.

You'll discover that some restoration work requires experimentation with different approaches, before you achieve the results you want. You won't achieve perfect results with every image; some will be too far damaged, and making the best attempt you can make will have to suffice. In most cases, you can still achieve pleasing results!

As mentioned earlier, if you are going to professionally restore and retouch photographs, skillful work will thrill your customers. That's why improving and maintaining your skill level is vital. There will be the occasional hard-to-please client, and there will be times when revising work will be necessary. While it's important to keep revisions to a minimum, they can also serve as learning experiences. Many times, I've learned a new and better way of restoring a photo because my first attempt wasn't satisfactory. After the revision, I'd end up with a very happy client—often leading to repeat business.

After you've spent a great deal of time editing a particularly difficult photo, it helps to leave it alone for a day or so and then reexamine it with a fresh set of eyes. (It also helps to have someone else look at it.) It can be frustrating to print your finished work only to discover it wasn't *quite* finished, because you overlooked something. After mastering the tutorials in this book, you might consider asking family and friends for practice photos. It's a great way to build a portfolio to show prospective clients. Just be sure to ask for permission to use them first—especially if you plan to put them online.

Equipment Purchases to Consider

These days, most people own a computer, scanner, and printer. All-in-one printer/copier/scanners are now quite common. These are the minimum equipment requirements for scanning, editing, and printing photographs up to 8" × 10". For many people, this will probably be sufficient. For those editing images at the serious amateur level or offering a professional service, there are a few other items to consider. They will make your workflow smoother and more efficient and will also enable you to handle a wider range of editing tasks. If you're a professional, you probably already have this equipment. If not, you might consider obtaining these:

- *A multiformat flatbed scanner* (Figure 6): Using a multiformat photo-quality scanner will capture images with a wide dynamic range (greater detail in shadow areas), as well as transparencies, such as 35mm slides and negatives. They typically range in price from about $100 for basic models to as much as $1200 for models that can scan 12–16 slides at one time.

Figure 6. *A multiformat flatbed scanner*

- *A good quality tripod*: You may encounter large images, such as 16" × 20" portraits. With a tripod and a good camera, you can digitize large images for editing. A decent consumer-quality camera will work, but a camera that captures in the RAW format is best. The tripod should have a head that tilts 90 degrees, so that the camera can be aimed straight down.

- *Lighting*: Digitizing large images outside on an overcast day works very well but may not always be possible. You can purchase from your local camera shop lighting equipment to illuminate large images. Photoflood bulbs emit light at 3200 or 3400 degrees Kelvin to work with your camera's indoor setting.

- *Graphics tablet* (Figure 7): A graphics tablet can make your work much easier and faster. It mimics the feel of using a brush, pencil, or pen. This is especially useful when applying colors to an image, such as colorizing a black-and-white photograph.

Figure 7. *A graphics tablet can make your work easier. (Image courtesy of Sasha Kim/Pexels)*

Copy with Caution

If you are learning the art of digital photo restoration for professional purposes, you'll have to be careful when duplicating and editing some images to avoid committing copyright infringement. Because I'm not an attorney, I can't really offer this as specific legal advice, but more as a general cautionary guide for you to keep in mind. *You should always consult an attorney who specializes in intellectual property law for legal specifics.*

On occasion, a customer will request retouching or modifying a professionally shot portrait. Legally, the photographer who took the picture owns the copyright to the image (unless other arrangements were agreed upon beforehand). When possible, have the customer obtain written permission from the photographer or studio that owns the copyright, before proceeding with any work. Naturally, some portraits will be decades old, and the photographer will have passed on or closed their business, or there simply may not be any way of knowing who the photographer is. In those cases, it's probably a moot issue.

It's good practice to have the customer sign a waiver (your attorney can help you draft one) releasing you from any copyright infringement liability. However, if the picture is obviously the work of a professional (especially a local photographer), obtaining permission to edit the image is very important. Photographers can be very protective of their work (trust me, I know), and you can't really blame them. If it happened to get back to them that you were editing their work, a lawsuit might follow. (I personally know of a photo lab owner who was almost sued over just such an incident.)

Many people believe that because they paid for the photography service and prints, they own the copyright to those images. It can sometimes be difficult to convey the concept that the photographer (or studio that employs them) owns the copyright. However, it's important that you do. Customers won't always understand why they need to obtain permission or sign a waiver, but you must legally protect yourself. It's also just professional courtesy to ask for permission to edit someone else's work.

So, be sure to remember these important points:

- When possible, have the customer sign a waiver releasing you from any potential copyright infringement. Most of the images you work with will be family snapshots or an old portrait that was the work of a professional. It may be impossible to identify the photographer.

- When it's obvious that a photo is the work of a professional, obtain permission from the copyright owner to edit the image, if at all possible. There is usually an embossed signature at the bottom-right corner of a photo and a "Do Not Copy" warning on the back.

- *Consult an attorney when you need more specific legal advice.* It pays to be careful.

Macintosh Users

The tutorials in this book use the Windows/Linux keyboard shortcuts, but if you are a Macintosh user unfamiliar with the Windows keyboard shortcuts, the Mac equivalents are shown in Table 1.

Table 1. *Mac/Windows Keyboard Shortcut Equivalents*

	Editing	
Function	**Mac OS**	**Windows**
Cut to clipboard	Command + X	Control + X
Copy to clipboard	Command + C	Control + C
Paste from clipboard	Command + V	Control + V
Undo	Command + Z	Control + Z
Contextual menus	Control-click	Right-click

Practice Images

You can download the Practice Images folder that contains the images that accompany each tutorial in this book. The images are contained in each corresponding subfolder. To download the Practice Images folder, download the source code package here: https://github.com/Apress/Beginning-Photo-Retouching-and-Restoration-Using-GIMP.

If you're ready now, you can start on your path to becoming an image retoucher and restoration artist!

PART I

Starting with the Essentials

CHAPTER 1

An Overview of GIMP 2.10

In This Chapter

- Downloading and Installing GIMP 2.10
- The GIMP Interface
- The Image Menu
- The Image Navigation Bar
- The Toolbox and Important Tool Functions
- Working with Layers
- Plug-ins to Enhance GIMP

Note If you are an absolute beginner, I hope that this chapter will provide you with enough information about GIMP to follow along with the exercises in this book. The GIMP *User Manual* will provide much more detailed information and can be accessed from the official GIMP website at www.gimp.org.

© Phillip Whitt 2023
P. Whitt, *Beginning Photo Retouching and Restoration Using GIMP*,
https://doi.org/10.1007/978-1-4842-9265-5_1

Downloading and Installing GIMP 2.10

If you don't already have GIMP installed on your computer, then the first thing to do is go to the official GIMP website at `www.gimp.org`. Next, just follow the following steps that apply to the operating system of your computer. Remember: GIMP is free—no need to have a credit card ready!

Once you are on the GIMP website, you'll see the Download button at the top of the home page (Figure 1-1). The GIMP website will automatically detect your computer's operating system. Click the Download button, and you'll be taken to the appropriate download link(s).

Figure 1-1. *The Download button on the GIMP home page*

GIMP for Windows

The following steps will help assist you in installing GIMP 2.10 on Windows:

1. Once you are on the *GIMP for Windows* page, you are offered a choice of downloading GIMP via BitTorrent, downloading directly (my preferred option), or from the Microsoft Store (Figure 1-2).

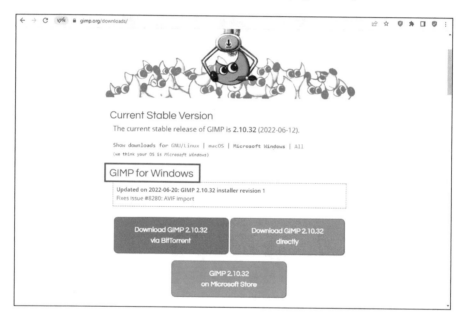

Figure 1-2. *GIMP for Windows can be downloaded via BitTorrent, directly, or from the Microsoft Store*

2. After the download completes, the GIMP installer will be in the Downloads folder (or the place you normally designate for downloads). Click the GIMP installer, and the *Open File-Security Warning* dialog

box will open. Click the *Run* button, and GIMP will be installed on your system. The installation process might take several minutes (Figure 1-3).

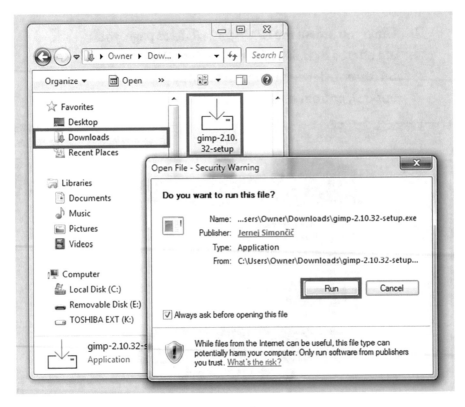

Figure 1-3. *Installing GIMP on Windows*

GIMP for Linux and Unix-Like Systems

Some Linux distributions may already have GIMP installed. If your version of Linux doesn't, there's usually a software repository that it can be downloaded from; Figure 1-4 shows GIMP in the software catalog for Zorin OS (a popular Linux distribution). When the icon is clicked, GIMP will be downloaded and installed on the system.

Figure 1-4. *GIMP can be acquired from the Linux distribution's software catalog*

GIMP for Mac OS X

This page (Figure 1-5) is where you'll find the download links for your Macintosh. You can now download the GIMP 2.10 installer via BitTorrent or directly.

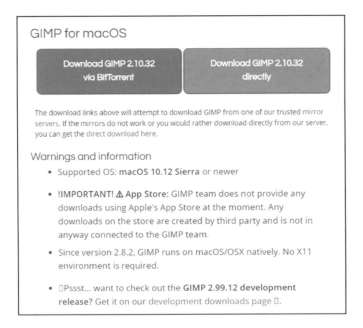

Figure 1-5. *GIMP for Mac OS X*

The current version of GIMP requires macOS 10.12 Sierra or newer.

The GIMP Interface

This is where it all happens—the digital darkroom where you'll learn how to retouch and restore your treasured images (or those of your clients). The interface may differ slightly in appearance from one platform to another, but the operations are pretty much the same across the board. Like many modern image-editing programs, GIMP sports a dark theme by default. In fact, it bears a strong resemblance to Adobe Photoshop's interface as shown in Figure 1-6.

Figure 1-6. *The GIMP interface*

The other themes are *Gray* and *Light*; to change Themes, go to *Edit* ➤ *Preferences*, and the Preferences dialog will open. Select *Theme* (from the left-hand panel) and choose the one you want to use (Figure 1-7).

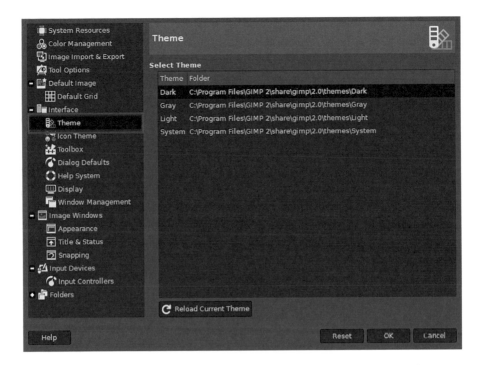

Figure 1-7. *You can choose a Theme from the Preferences dialog*

There are several Icon Themes available as well, *Symbolic* being the default. The others are *Color, Legacy, Symbolic-High Contrast, Symbolic-Inverted,* and *Symbolic-Inverted-High Contrast.* To change Icon Themes, go to Edit ➤ Preferences, and the Preferences dialog will open. Select *Icon Theme* (from the left-hand panel) and choose the one you want to use (Figure 1-8).

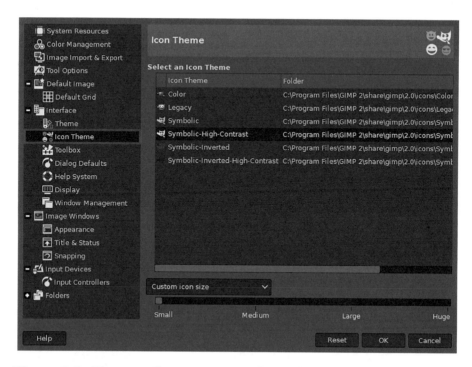

Figure 1-8. *You can choose an Icon Theme from the Preferences dialog*

GIMP launches in the *Single-Window* mode by default (all of the docks and image window are unified). GIMP can also be used in the *Multi-Window* mode; in this mode, the panels and image window are separate and can be moved around if needed (this is especially useful when screen space is limited).

To change from the Single Window to Multi-Window mode, select Windows ➤ Single-Window, then click in the box to disable the Single-Window mode (Figure 1-9). GIMP will now operate in the Multi-Window mode. If you're new to GIMP, I recommend trying both modes to see which one you're more comfortable using.

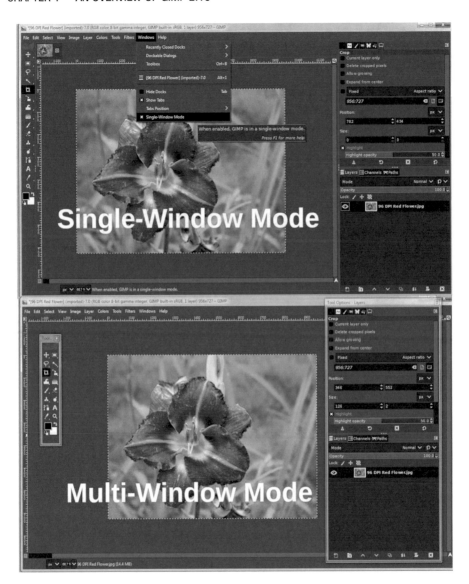

Figure 1-9. *A comparison of the Single-Window and Multi-Window modes*

The Image Menu

The *Image Menu* is located above the GIMP image window (under the Title bar). Figure 1-10 shows the *Colors Menu* being accessed from the Image Menu. The Image Menu can be thought of as "Command Headquarters"; you can access almost every function from here. The following is a quick run-through of some (but not all) of the functions within each option:

- *File*: Opens existing files, creates new files, saves, and exports

- *Edit*: Undoes and redoes, copies, pastes, and accesses preferences

- *Select*: Provides various options for choosing and modifying selections

- *View*: Provides viewing options for images, layers, navigation, and guides

- *Image*: Provides options for adjusting image orientation, size, printing images, and canvas settings

- *Layer*: Creates new layers, duplicates existing layers, and works with layer properties

- *Colors*: Accesses the color adjustment dialogs, such as Color Balance, Levels, Curves, and Hue/Saturation

- *Tools*: Accesses the image-editing and color tools

- *Filters*: Accesses the filters, such as Blur or Sharpen, as well as artistic and specialty filters

- *Windows*: Accesses the recently closed docks, hiding docks, etc.

- *Help*: Accesses the GIMP *User Manual* (if installed on your computer) and also links to the online GIMP *User Manual*

Many of the functions used routinely have keyboard shortcuts. It's a good idea to familiarize yourself with them and make a habit of using them on a regular basis; this will help you work faster and more efficiently.

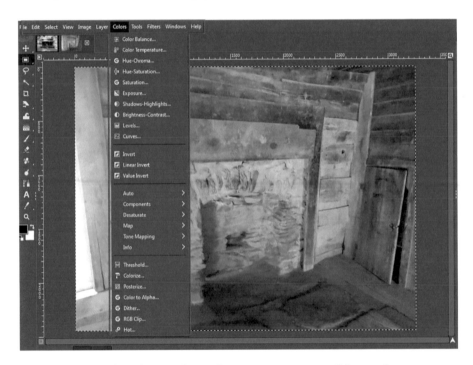

Figure 1-10. *This shows the Colors Menu accessed from the Image Menu*

The Image Navigation Bar

This is a useful new feature for GIMP 2.10. The Image Navigation Bar allows you to easily browse through all of the images that are open in GIMP, by viewing the thumbnail images just above the image workspace (Figure 1-11).

Simply click the thumbnail of the image you want to display in the workspace. The thumbnail of the active image displays a *Close View* box to the right.

Figure 1-11. *Image Navigation Bar*

The Toolbox and Important Tool Functions

The Toolbox groups many of the functions you'll use on a routine basis. To identify each tool, hold the cursor over the icon and the tool name. A brief description of its function and the keyboard shortcut pop up in a small callout (the Perspective Clone tool doesn't use a keyboard shortcut). When a tool is active, the Tool Options dialog is also displayed (Figure 1-12).

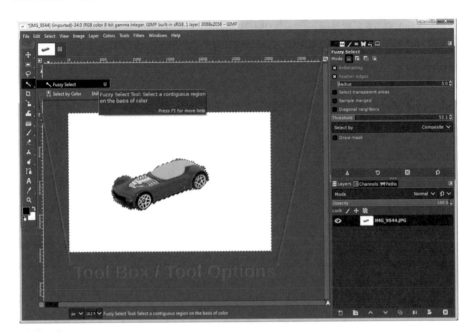

Figure 1-12. *The Toolbox and the Tool Options dialog*

The Selection Tools

GIMP offers a variety of selection tools that will enable you to isolate certain areas of the image you're editing. This confines the changes you want to make to the pixels within the selection boundary, leaving the rest of the image unaltered. The Free Select tool is one of the most commonly used selection tools, allowing you to draw an outline around the area you want to isolate. The Fuzzy Select tool is useful for isolating regions by color range (Figure 1-13).

Figure 1-13. *An example of a freehand selection and a selection by color range*

Selections can be further refined with the Quick Mask function, which will be explored further later on. You'll be able to edit selections with great precision, which is useful for isolating people to put on different backgrounds or to recompose images. Refer to Table 1-1 to become familiar with the name, shortcut, and function of each tool.

Table 1-1. *Tool Shortcuts and Functions*

Icon	Name	Shortcut	Tool Function
▣	Rectangle	R	Selects rectangular or square areas
◉	Ellipse	E	Selects elliptical or circular areas
◒	Free Select	F	Draws free-form and polygonal selections
◤	Fuzzy Select	U	Selects continuous areas of color
▦	Select By Color	Shift + O	Selects areas of similar color
✂	Intelligent Scissors	I	Selects shapes, using intelligent edge fitting
▣	Foreground Select	*(none)*	Selects an area with foreground objects

The Brush Tools

The brush tools (brushes) in GIMP allow you to paint, repair flaws, and apply local exposure corrections, among other things. Out of all of the brushes (for the purposes of retouching and restoration), the "dynamic duo" of the set would be the Clone tool and the Healing tool. These are the two you'll most often use to correct imperfections and repair damage on the images you edit (Figure 1-14).

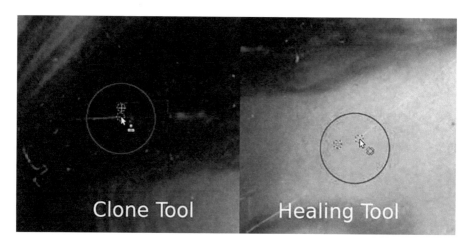

Figure 1-14. *Repairing damage with the Clone tool and the Healing tool*

The Clone tool works by sampling the pixels from one part of an image and pasting them on a target area on another part. The Healing tool is a type of "smart clone" that takes the surrounding texture and tone of the sampled area into account and seamlessly blends the pixels in for a flawless repair. Generally, the Clone tool is better suited to repairing larger cracks and creases, and the Healing tool, although it can be good at repairing smaller cracks and creases, is usually best at removing facial blemishes in portrait retouching.

There are plenty of other tools you'll be using in your retouching and restoration exercises. Table 1-2 briefly describes each tool with its keyboard shortcut and function.

Table 1-2. *Tool Shortcuts and Functions*

Icon	Name	Shortcut	Tool Function
	Bucket Fill	Shift + B	Fills an area with a color or a pattern
	Gradient	G	Fills an area with a gradient
	Pencil	N	Draws hard-edged lines
	Paintbrush	P	Paints smooth strokes using a brush nib
	Eraser	Shift + E	Removes pixels from a layer
	Airbrush	A	Paints using variable pressure, similar to a paint spray gun
	Ink	K	Calligraphy-style painting
	MyPaint Brush	Y	Use MyPaint Brushes in GIMP
	Clone	C	Copies pixels from one part of an image to another
	Healing	H	Heals image irregularities by blending in surrounding texture and tone
	Perspective Clone	*(none)*	Clone from an image source, after applying perspective transformation
	Blur/Sharpen	Shift + U	Selective blurring or sharpening, using a brush
	Smudge	S	Selective smudging, using a brush
	Dodge/Burn	Shift + D	Selective lightening or darkening, using a brush

The Transform Tools

The Transform tools allow you to alter the size, position, orientation, and perspective of the image and individual layers or selected areas. These features are extremely useful for recomposting images, straightening crooked images, correcting lens distortion, etc. The two examples shown in Figure 1-15 are *Rotate* and *Scale*.

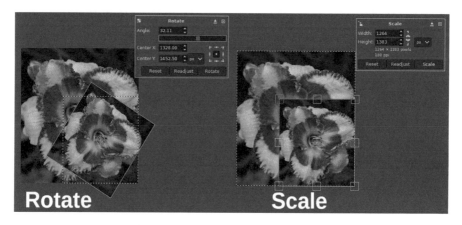

Figure 1-15. *Two examples of Transform tools*

Another example would be using the *Perspective* tool to correct the distortion that often results when photographing a building—an exercise we'll undertake later in this book. Refer to Table 1-3 to become familiar with the name, shortcut, and function of each tool.

Table 1-3. *Tool Shortcuts and Functions*

Icon	Name	Shortcut	Tool Function
	Move	M	Moves layers and selections
	Align	Q	Aligns or arranges layers and other objects
	Crop	Shift + C	Removes edge areas from the image or layer
	Unified Transform	Shift + T	Transforms the layer, selection, or path
	Rotate	Shift + R	Rotates the active layer, selection, or path
	Scale	Shift + S	Scales the active layer, selection, or path
	Shear	Shift + H	Shears the active layer, selection, or path
	Perspective	Shift + P	Changes the perspective of the active layer, selection, or path
	Flip	Shift + F	Reverses layers, selections, or paths vertically or horizontally
	3D Transform	Shift + W	Applies a 3D transformation to a layer, selection, or path
	Handle Transform	Shift + L	Deforms the layer, selection, or path with handles

Other Tools

The remaining tools are the Path tool, Color Picker, Zoom tool, Measure tool, and the Text tool. Power GIMP users employ all the tools in the Toolbox at one time or another, and the exercises in this book will use most of them at least once.

If you are accustomed to using Photoshop, the tools should seem somewhat familiar, but the names and icons might differ slightly. Refer to Table 1-4 to become familiar with the name, shortcut, and function of each tool.

Table 1-4. *Tool Shortcuts and Functions*

Icon	Name	Shortcut	Tool Function
🔲	Path	B	Creates and modifies paths
🔲	Color Picker	O	Selects colors from image pixels
🔲	Zoom	Z	Adjusts the magnification level of the image you are viewing
🔲	Measure	Shift + M	Shows distances and angles
🔲	Text	T	Creates or edits text layers

Working with Layers

Layers can be thought of as sheets of clear acetate, each one with a graphical element stacked on top of another. The sample illustration shown in Figure 1-16 demonstrates how the elements on each layer combine to form a complete composite image.

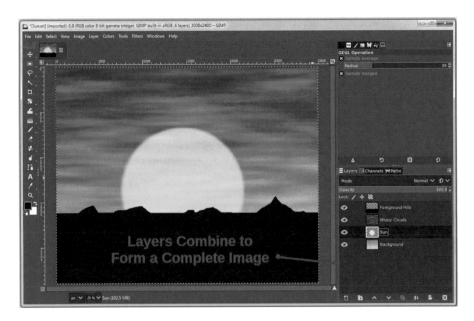

Figure 1-16. *Separate layers form a complete picture*

Layers are one of the most important aspects of image editing. Sometimes, it will be necessary to make revisions to your work, and having a layered version will make this much easier. For example, if I decided to remove the sun from the previous image, I can simply delete that layer (Figure 1-17).

Figure 1-17. *Individual layers can be deleted or edited without affecting the rest of the image*

A word of caution: You should *never edit directly on the background layer*! In the example shown in Figure 1-18, a new layer has been added, and the cloning is done on this layer instead of the original background layer.

Figure 1-18. *Editing on a separate layer protects the original background layer*

You might end up having numerous layers in your restoration projects, depending on the degree of work involved. It's a good practice to name the layers as you create them. If you have a project with many layers, it will make it much easier to find a particular layer, should you need to edit it.

Layer Groups

Layer groups were introduced in GIMP 2.8 and are very helpful for organizing large numbers of layers to edit. Clicking the small plus/minus box next to the Layer Group thumbnail will reveal or hide the layer preview thumbnails (Figure 1-19). This will help make your work go smoother when you work with complex images composed of a large number of layers.

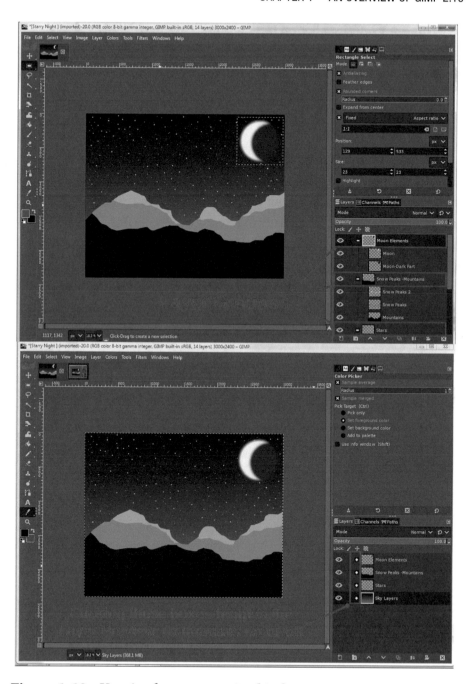

Figure 1-19. *Keeping layers organized in layer groups*

This book only touches on layer groups. For more detailed information, refer to the GIMP User Manual: `https://docs.gimp.org/en/gimp-layer-groups.html`.

Layer Blending Modes

Layers have a variety of *blending modes*, which interact with the underlying layer in specific ways. Blending modes can be very useful when restoring photos. For example, an underexposed photo, such as the one in Figure 1-20, can be quickly enhanced by simply duplicating the background layer and changing the blending mode to Screen. The result is a brighter picture.

It's often possible to correct images with serious tonal problems with a combination of blending modes. It will require some experimentation but can often work very well.

Figure 1-20. *Layer blend modes improve the tonal quality of this image*

Plug-ins to Enhance GIMP

There are a number of plug-ins for GIMP that expand its capabilities. Some plug-ins are useful, some not so much, at least for photo restoration work. Unfortunately, the GIMP Plugin Registry is no longer maintained. GIMP plug-ins are still available; they're just scattered around on the Internet.

Fortunately, there is a photography website called Shotkit that offers an installation guide that can be found here: `https://shotkit.com/gimp-plugins/`. It will help you obtain 18 of the best plug-ins for GIMP.

Summary

We looked at how to download and install GIMP 2.10 on your computer and had a cursory overview of the software. As mentioned earlier, the overview will help you to get acquainted with GIMP, but you also have access to the *GIMP User Manual*, which covers everything about this program in depth.

For the absolute beginner using GIMP, the best way to learn this program is by jumping in and spending time playing with it. Of course, the book *Practical Glimpse* (Apress Publishing) covers the program Glimpse, which is virtually identical to GIMP and is a useful guide for beginners.

I would encourage you to open an image (make a copy of it first) and use the tools to see what they do and how they behave. Experiment with the functions in the Image Menu to see how they work. When you do the tutorials in this book, step-by-step guidance is provided. After you've become somewhat acquainted with GIMP, feel free to move on to Chapter 2.

CHAPTER 2

Digitizing Your Photos, Slides, and Negatives

In This Chapter

- Acquiring Your Digital Images

- Starting with a Clean Scan

- Scanning Photographs

- Digitizing Large Images

- Scanning Slides and Negatives

- Straightening and Cropping Your Images

Acquiring Your Digital Images

As you're mastering the exercises in this book, you might be eager to try your newly acquired skills on your own images. Getting your images into a digital format is the first step toward the image-editing process. You can

© Phillip Whitt 2023
P. Whitt, *Beginning Photo Retouching and Restoration Using GIMP*,
https://doi.org/10.1007/978-1-4842-9265-5_2

either hire the task out or do it yourself—which, I presume, will be the choice of the majority of those reading this book.

If you are going to work only with relatively small photographic prints (8" × 10" or less), a basic model scanner will be adequate. If you plan to digitize transparencies such as slides and negatives, you'll need a *multiformat* flatbed scanner. These models will digitize transparencies as well as photos. Some models will handle medium- and large-format negatives, such as 4" × 5". There are also dedicated scanners for digitizing mounted slides (in a 2" × 2" mount) and 35mm negatives.

A tripod and good digital camera are useful tools for digitizing large images, as you'll see shortly. You'll be able to comfortably digitize portraits up to 16" × 20".

Starting with a Clean Scan

Because it's likely that the image you are scanning requires some type of digital repair, it's logical to assume that you don't want to add even more dreck to remove. I make it a habit to keep a can of compressed air (or a bulb brush), a can of foam-type glass cleaner, and a clean cloth near my scanner (Figure 2-1). There's no need to digitally edit out a small hair or stray ball of dust from your image, when you can avoid scanning it in the first place. It's also a good idea to use a soft bristle brush or bulb brush on the material to be scanned, to remove any loose dust. This is especially true with transparencies—even the smallest dust particles will stand out. Use caution when brushing off original materials. If the emulsion is flaking or loose, you could make the damage even worse.

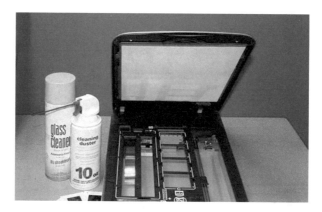

Figure 2-1. *Keeping cleaning articles near your scanner is a good idea*

Note   When cleaning your scanner, spray the cleaning fluid on the cloth and not on the glass platen. This will prevent the cleaning fluid from running into the seams of your scanner, which could possibly damage it.

Scanning Photographs

It's important to scan the original image at the correct resolution to have sufficient data to work with, especially when the edited image will be printed as an enlargement. If the input data is too low, the result will be an image with a jagged appearance. The illustration in Figure 2-2 shows two enlarged sections scanned from a 3" × 5" photograph of the lettering on a boat. The image on the left is a scan at 300 DPI (for print), and that on the right is a scan at 75 DPI (the resolution generally used for viewing images on the Web). Ninety-six DPI is also used for web-based images.

Figure 2-2. *A comparison of 300 DPI and 75 DPI scans*

Generally, scanning a photograph at 300 DPI is sufficient, if the final print output size doesn't exceed the original image size—at least, by very much. When you upscale an image, the software must *interpolate*, or estimate, when it adds pixels to re-create the image data. Without sufficient captured image data, an enlarged photo will look horrible when printed.

My clients often request enlargements made from small prints. These can be achieved (within reason) by scanning the original at a higher resolution. I find that scanning a small print (such as one that is wallet size) at 600–800 DPI will usually suffice, depending on the image quality you are starting with and how much you want to enlarge the image (8" × 10" is about the maximum I will attempt to coax from a wallet-size original).

After performing the necessary edits, the file can be scaled up to the desired output size. For printing, the image can be downsampled to 300 DPI.

Digitizing Large Images

Most of the images you scan will be small enough to fit comfortably on a scanning bed that accommodates a sheet 8.5" × 11". But what if you are confronted with an old 16" × 20" portrait? If you have large photographs to contend with, there are options available to enable you to digitize them, in order to transfer them to your computer, so that you can edit them.

Find a Service Provider

When you have to digitize a large photograph, check with the local photo labs or with photographers who offer copy services. They can photograph your image and either provide you with a copy negative or a digital file (which is preferable). Printing companies often use oversized scanners for large documents, photographs, or artwork—usually up to 11" × 17".

Use Your Camera and Tripod

With a sturdy tripod and a decent digital camera, you can fashion your own copy stand to digitize large pictures (you can also purchase a purpose-built copy stand from a photographic supplier). The tripod should have a head that can tilt at 90 degrees and be tall enough to allow adequate room to place the image between the feet. I set up the example in Figure 2-3 outside, on an overcast day, with my camera's white balance set to Daylight and the ISO set to 100. Although I prefer shooting outside like this, it's not always practical—the weather doesn't always cooperate.

For working indoors, good results can be achieved by using three or four 250-watt photoflood lamps and the Tungsten setting on your camera. Photoflood bulbs have a color temperature of 3200 degrees Kelvin to help capture your image with the correct color balance. B&H Photo is a great online supplier from which to purchase studio lighting equipment. Visit their site at `www.bhphotovideo.com`. You can also shop on eBay for good used equipment.

Figure 2-3. *A tripod set up as a copy stand and a 16" × 20" portrait digitized with a camera*

The following are the steps to capture a large image with a digital camera and tripod setup:

1. Position the tripod over the image.

2. Tilt the tripod's head at a 90-degree angle (the camera should point straight down at the image) and move the tripod, as required, to frame the image within the camera's viewfinder and minimize distortion of the image.

3. If you're working inside, make sure the image is evenly illuminated.

4. Adjust the camera's white balance, if your camera has manual settings; otherwise, use the auto white balance.

5. Make sure the image is in focus, and capture it with your camera. Experiment with the ISO and exposure settings and capture several variations of the image, so that you can then choose the best one.

6. Capture the image with the highest quality setting possible. The more image data you capture the better.

7. The image might have some slight keystone distortion. After you import the file to your computer, use GIMP's Perspective transform tool to correct the distortion (Figure 2-4). A plug-in worth trying to help correct lens distortions is GimpLensfun, available from `https://lensfun.github.io/`.

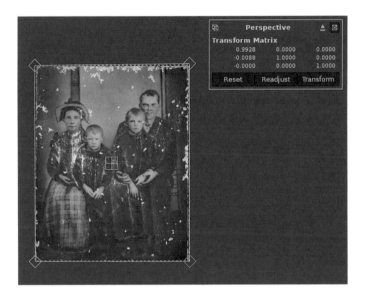

Figure 2-4. *Using the Perspective tool to correct distortion*

Tip   Images with a glossy or reflective surface might need to be propped up on one side, so they're not lying perfectly flat. This will angle the surface of an image to eliminate any glare that might show up in the captured copy.

Scanning Photos in Sections

An alternative to using a camera and tripod setup is to scan larger photos in sections. This method is better suited for photos that can be scanned in two sections, such as a 10" × 13" or an 11" × 14" print. It also works well for panoramas that have been rolled up for many years and are too curled to lay flat for using the camera-tripod capture method.

The following sample 11" × 14" image is included (ch2_babygirl.jpg, parts 1 and 2) in the Practice Images folder. If you don't have a photograph that large to scan, at least you can follow along the reassembly portion of this tutorial using the practice images.

The following are the steps to capture an 11" × 14" image by scanning it in two sections:

1. Lay one end of the photograph horizontally across the scanning bed.

2. Scan the image at 300 DPI into GIMP (Image Menu ➤ *File Create* ➤ *Scanner/Camera*). Select your scanner when prompted. Expand the canvas (Image Menu ➤ *Image* ➤ *Canvas Size*) to about 4500 pixels (15") wide. This will give you some extra wiggle room to negotiate the second part of the image into place (Figure 2-5).

3. Rename the background layer Scan 1 (Activate the Background Layer ➤ right-click ➤ Edit Layer Attributes).

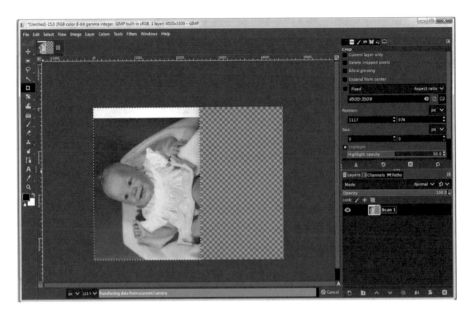

Figure 2-5. *The background expanded on the first part of the scanned image*

4. Lay the other end of the photograph horizontally across the scanning bed, keeping the orientation the same as the first scan. Scan it into GIMP (Figure 2-6).

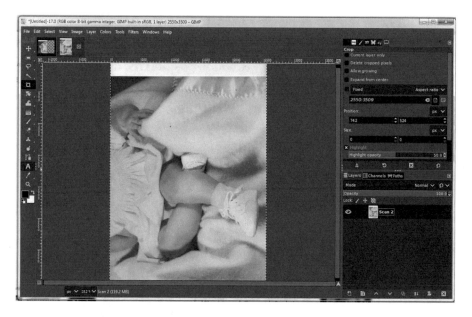

Figure 2-6. *The second part of the image scanned into GIMP*

5. Copy the image to the clipboard (Image Menu ➤ Edit ➤ *Copy*).

6. Activate the first scanned image by clicking the tab on the *Image Navigation Bar*.

7. Paste the second part of the image (Image Menu ➤ Edit ➤ Paste As New Layer).

8. Change the layer's boundary size to match the image size (Layer ➤ right-click ➤ Layer to Image Size).

9. Rename the layer Scan 2.

10. Lower the layer's opacity enough to see the first scan underneath. This will help make alignment easier (Figure 2-7). Using the Move tool, position the layer into place and use the Arrow keys to nudge it in small increments, for precise alignment.

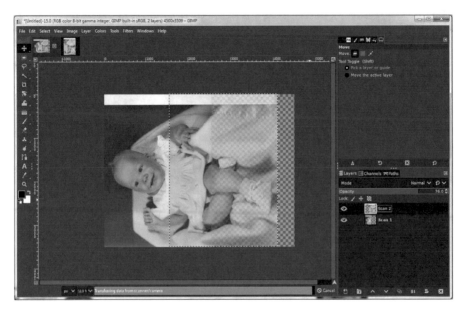

Figure 2-7. *Position the second part of the image into place*

11. After the second part is in position, increase the layer's opacity back up to 100%.

12. There is usually a visible line and some tonal difference running along the image, similar to the example being used in this guide. To remove this, add a Layer Mask to the layer named Scan 2 (right-click ➤ Add Layer Mask). Use the default White (Full Opacity) setting.

13. Activate the Paintbrush tool. Using a large, soft brush and black as the active color, paint away the line (Figure 2-8). Depending on the results you achieve with your image, it might be necessary to vary the brush opacity.

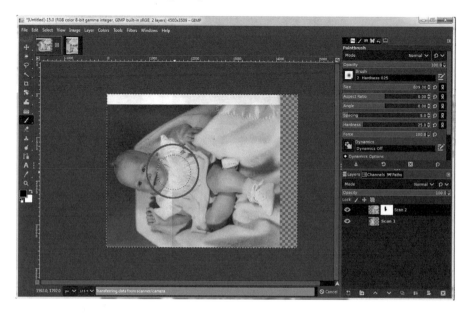

Figure 2-8. *Removing the line and tonal differences with a large, soft brush*

14. After the two sections match to your satisfaction, use the *Crop tool* to trim away the excess area. Rotate the image to its proper vertical position (*Image Menu ➤ Image ➤ Transform ➤ Rotate 90 Degrees Clockwise*).

15. Save a layered copy as an XCF file, which is GIMP's native file format. It's always a good practice to save layered copies, in case you have to make revisions.

16.   Flatten the image. If it requires restoration work, this will become the background layer. Save this version with a new name. You now have the image digitized and can move forward with its restoration (Figure 2-9).

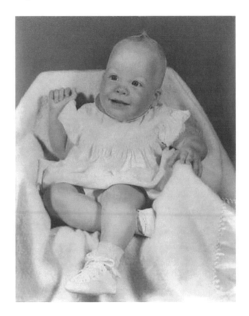

Figure 2-9. *The two parts unified into a complete image*

Scanning Slides and Negatives

The vast majority of your retouching and restoration tasks will involve working from photographic prints. Of course, transparencies can incur damage over time—mold and mildew, embedded dirt, and color shifts are fairly common. It might be a good idea to hire this task out if you rarely come into contact with transparencies and don't want to invest in a dedicated or multiformat scanner. On the other hand, if photo-editing work will be part of your professional activities, then investing in a capable scanner would be a wise choice. Digitizing slides and negatives can add a boost to your income stream. A multiformat flatbed scanner offers added versatility. You'll be able to obtain good scans from a variety of original photographic materials. These scanners use *adapters* to hold the transparencies in place on the scanner's bed (Figure 2-10). A high-quality, dedicated slide/negative scanner can offer the ultimate in quality scans, with the best *dynamic range* (detail in shadow areas). It pays to do some research to best determine your needs before making your purchase.

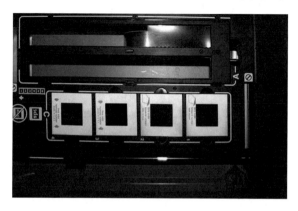

Figure 2-10. *The adapter used for scanning 2" × 2" mounted slides and 35mm negatives*

Before You Start

Remember the rule about starting with a clean scan? This is *especially* important when transparencies are involved. Every speck of dust and dirt shows up in a scan. A blower brush and a clean, lint-free cloth should be used to remove as much loose dust from transparencies as possible. It's amazing how much you can reduce your workload simply by cleaning the transparency first, as well as making sure the scanner is clean. Figure 2-11 illustrates this point well. Notice the difference between the two scans of a 35mm color negative. Using a clean, lint-free cloth makes a huge improvement. Now it requires only minimal digital cleanup work. Of course, the results will vary: some transparencies will have more embedded dirt and dust than others. Film cleaning fluids are available but should be used with great care and *lots* of ventilation, as the fumes these fluids give off can be flammable, as well as dangerous if breathed for prolonged periods.

Figure 2-11. *Cleaning this negative with a lint-free cloth makes a huge difference*

Using the Auto-Settings

Normally, I don't use the scanner's automated features. I prefer to capture the image as close to original as possible.

However, some of the auto-settings can be expedient when scanning large quantities of slides or negatives and time is limited. I find the most useful are the color-correction and exposure-correction features. The dyes in slides often fade and change over time, and the images have often been shot at the wrong exposure. Figure 2-12 illustrates the improvement made in a 126 color slide taken in the 1960s. The image isn't perfect, but it is a far cry from what it was.

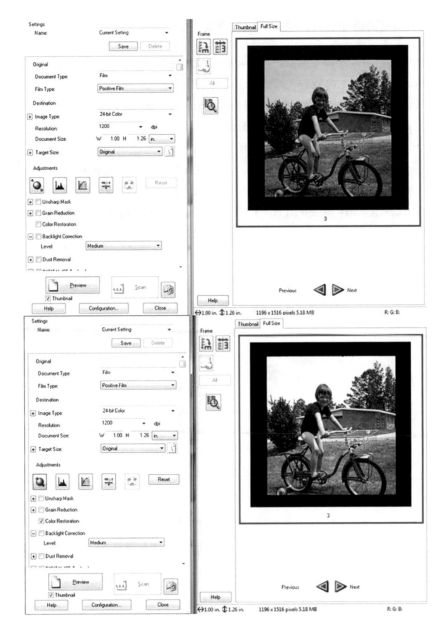

Figure 2-12. *The auto color feature improves this 126 color slide*

Note   While the aforementioned auto-settings can be time savers and work well, beware of ones such as Digital ICE or other dust-removal features. They can soften the image, resulting in diminished quality. The best action is to remove as much physical dust as possible before scanning. If you must use a dust-removal feature, try using minimal settings.

Scanning Resolution for Transparencies

What resolution should you scan your slides and negatives? The answer is, it depends. Many of my clients no longer have a working slide projector but would like to be able to see their slides again. Usually, they want to view them as a slide show on their television or computer monitor. For that purpose, scanning them at an ultra-high resolution isn't required. I find that scanning them at 400–600 DPI works well for viewing on a monitor or television screen, particularly in high definition.

However, the best option is scanning at a resolution to provide the highest-quality image data. I normally scan them at a *minimum* of 1200 DPI while scaling up to 4" × 6" for 35mm slides and negatives and 6" × 6" for 126 slides. Scanning at 2400 DPI or more is a better option if the image will be printed at 8" × 10" or larger. Most modern scanners are capable of resolutions well beyond 2400 DPI.

The reality is that scanning at such a high resolution creates a large file size, but you are capturing sufficient image data to provide adequate image quality. Trying to get a decent 8" × 10" print from a slide scanned at 300 DPI will only disappoint. Looking at the enlarged example, it's easy to see how much more jagged the leaf on the left is from a 300 DPI scan compared to the same leaf from a 1200 DPI scan, both taken from the same 35mm color negative (Figure 2-13).

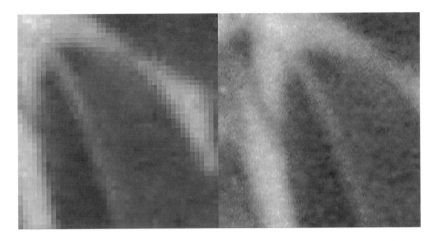

Figure 2-13. *An enlarged section of a 300 DPI scan compared to one at 1200 DPI, from a 35mm color negative*

Straightening and Cropping Your Images

The images you work with will sometimes require straightening out by leveling the horizon line. Sometimes, the original photograph has an irregular shape, and squaring it perfectly on the scanner's bed is difficult, at best. Other times, the photographer may just have held the camera at an odd angle, resulting in a crooked image. The following are the steps to straighten an image in GIMP:

1. Scan the image into GIMP (*Image Menu ➤ File ➤ Create ➤ Scanner/Camera*). Select your scanner when prompted. The following sample image (ch2_tilted ocean.jpg) is also included in the Practice Images available for download from the Apress companion web page (mentioned in the Introduction), if you'd like to use it to follow along.

2. Select the *Rotate tool* (Shift + R). Set the angle to 4.10 (Figure 2-14).

Figure 2-14. *A Horizontal Guide can be used to assist you when leveling the image*

3. Now the image is straightened—and is starting to look better (Figure 2-15).

Figure 2-15. *The image is now straightened*

4.   Next, select the *Crop tool* (Shift + C) and trim away the excess area around the image. Compared to the before example, it now looks much better (Figure 2-16).

Figure 2-16. *A before-and-after comparison*

Summary

In this chapter, you learned that acquiring your photographic materials as digital images is the first step in the editing process, so it should be done as well as possible. There are choices as to whether to hire this task out or do it yourself, depending on what best suits you. When scanning your own photographic prints, dust removal is important, as is acquiring sufficient image data by scanning at the right resolution.

With a good tripod (or copy stand) and camera, you can digitize large images. It's also possible to scan some larger photos in sections and to reassemble them as complete images.

Transparencies require an especially high degree of dust and dirt removal, because everything is captured by the scanner. Auto-settings, while not always ideal, can speed up the process of handling large quantities of transparencies. You also discovered that transparencies requiring high-resolution scanning capture the maximum image data.

Images will sometimes have to be straightened out after scanning, because of having an irregular shape or being shot at odd angles in the first place.

GIMP can easily fix tilted images and much, much more, as you'll see as we proceed into Part II of this book.

PART II

Tone, Exposure, and Color

CHAPTER 3

Correcting Tone and Exposure

In This Chapter

- Common Tonal Problems
- The Brightness-Contrast Dialog
- Tonal Corrections Using Levels
- Tonal Corrections Using Curves
- Tonal Corrections Using Layer Modes

Common Tonal Problems

Many old photographs have various tonal problems—low contrast, loss of detail from fading, darkening with age, etc. Even many of the pictures you currently shoot with your digital camera could probably benefit from tonal corrections. Sometimes, one or two adjustments are all that is needed to revive a dull photograph. Other problems will require a greater degree of correction.

© Phillip Whitt 2023
P. Whitt, *Beginning Photo Retouching and Restoration Using GIMP*,
https://doi.org/10.1007/978-1-4842-9265-5_3

Many, if not most, of the images you work with will require some degree of tonal adjustment. Tonal problems generally fall under one of the following descriptions:

- The image is overexposed/too bright.

- The image is underexposed/too dark.

- The image has low contrast/dull and flat.

Some images have local or mixed tonal issues. For example, an image might be properly exposed in one area and underexposed in another.

Using the Histogram to Assess Tonality

A *histogram* (Figure 3-1) is a graphical representation of the pixel brightness values in an image, ranging from 0 (pure black) to 255 (pure white). Factors such as image tonality and exposure determine the shape of the histogram. Tonal correction tools such as Levels and Curves display a histogram in the window. You can also access the histogram window by itself (Image Menu ➤ Colors ➤ Info ➤ Histogram).

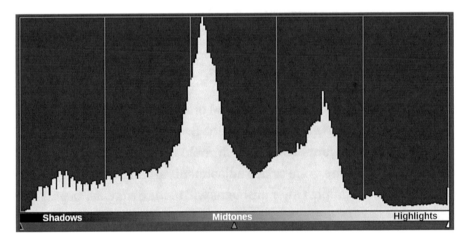

Figure 3-1. *A histogram represents pixel brightness in the image data*

You can look at an image and tell whether it's too bright, too dark, etc. Viewing the histogram will show you how the image data is distributed within the image. This information is important for making the proper tonal correction, as you'll see in more depth in the upcoming "Tonal Corrections Using Levels" section of the chapter.

The following examples demonstrate how the image tone distributes the data in a histogram:

- *Overexposed (too bright)*: Most of the image data is in the mid-range to the bright pixels in the histogram (Figure 3-2).

Figure 3-2. *Most of the data is in the brightest range*

- *Underexposed (too dark)*: Most of the image data is in the mid-range to the dark pixels in the histogram (Figure 3-3).

Figure 3-3. *Most of the data is in the darkest range*

- *Low contrast (dull tone)*: Most of the image data is in the mid-range, with none in the darkest or lightest ranges (Figure 3-4).

Figure 3-4. *Most of the data is in the middle range*

- *Balanced tonality*: The image data is spread across the full length of the histogram (Figure 3-5).

Figure 3-5. *Most of the data is spread throughout the histogram*

Tonal problems could be due to improper lighting or exposure settings or, in the case of old photographs, chemical changes in the print itself over time. Old photographs will often have mixed tonal issues, such as uneven fading, which can make correction more complex and challenging.

Using the Color Picker Tool to Track Tonality

As mentioned in the Introduction, software to calibrate your monitor can be very helpful to display an image as accurately as possible. However, it's a good idea to take measurements for an accurate readout of what pixel values you are seeing. What you see on your monitor may differ some from reality.

The Color Picker tool is used to sample areas to determine color values and tonal values. In the grayscale image in Figure 3-6, an area of sky has been sampled to determine the gray value (percentages). A grayscale image (as displayed on a monitor) is made up of equal amounts of red, green, and blue light—in this case, the area sample is 95%, which translates to 5% gray. Using the eyedropper to sample pixels will display the brightness value from 0 to 255 and also the RGB values. You can sample a single pixel or an average of a radius of pixels you set the parameters for.

Figure 3-6. *Using the Color Picker tool to track tonality*

Using Sample Points

Sample Points are markers that can be placed on various parts of an image to help monitor specific areas as you edit. The data displayed will change in real time as you work. They can be used to keep track of highlights, midtones, and shadows throughout the image (Figure 3-7). They are useful when making tonal changes and show you certain areas that may be adversely affected, allowing you to selectively fine-tune those areas. Although this book doesn't delve into using Sample Points in the tutorials, you may find them helpful as your image-editing skills advance.

Figure 3-7. *Tracking image data using Sample Points*

You can access the Sample Points dialog from the Image menu (Windows ➤ Dockable Dialogs ➤ Sample Points). To create a Sample Point, Control-click one of the rulers in the image window, and drag with the mouse. Two perpendicular guides will appear. When you release the mouse button, the Sample Point will be placed where the two guides intersect (Figure 3-8).

Figure 3-8. *Creating a Sample Point*

The Exposure Dialog

The *Exposure* dialog is used to make quick improvements in images that are underexposed. The dialog essentially adjusts the image's black level and relative brightness in stops.

Figure 3-9 shows the dialog and provides a brief description of the settings (except the bottom four, which are self-explanatory):

1. *Presets*: Pick a preset from the list.

2. *Save the current settings as named preset.*

3. *Manage presets.*

4. *Black level*: Adjust the black level.

5. *Exposure*: Relative brightness change in stops.

6. *Blending Options*: Opens and closes the Mode menu.

7. *Mode*: This menu contains a variety of blend modes.

8. *Switch to another group of modes*: Switches between legacy (older GIMP) blend modes and current blend modes.

9. *Opacity*: Reduces the effect by lowering the opacity.

10. *Split view*: Provides a split before-and-after view before the action is committed.

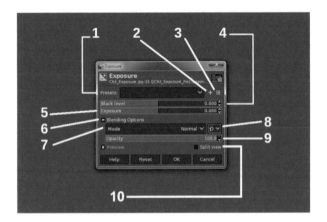

Figure 3-9. *The Exposure dialog*

Tutorial 1: Using the Exposure Dialog

In this exercise, we'll use the Exposure dialog to brighten up an underexposed image that's a bit too dark (Figure 3-10).

Figure 3-10. *An underexposed image that will be corrected using the Exposure dialog*

To correct this image, follow these steps:

1. Open the image (*Ch3_Exposure_Fix*) found in the Practice Images folder.

2. Duplicate the background layer (Shift + Control + D) and rename it Exposure Fix (Figure 3-11)—it's always advisable to work on a separate layer.

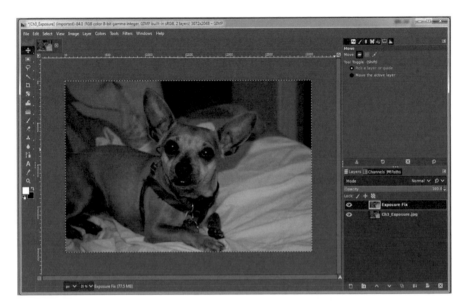

Figure 3-11. *Duplicate the background layer and rename it Exposure Fix*

3.   Open the Histogram dialog (Windows ➤ Dockable Dialogs ➤ Histogram); this will graphically display the tonal information.

4.   Open the Exposure dialog (Colors ➤ Exposure).

5.   As shown in Figure 3-12, set the Exposure slider to 1.42—you can see the tonal information in the Histogram being remapped as the Exposure adjustment is made.

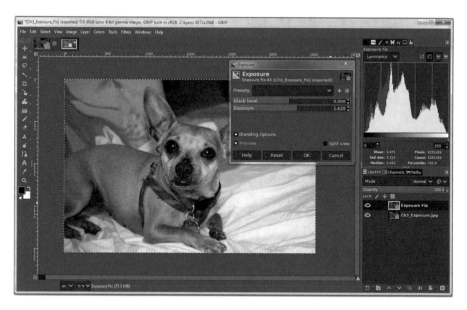

Figure 3-12. *Set the Exposure slider to 1.42 and click OK*

In the before-and-after comparison, we can see the image looks brighter and cleaner (Figure 3-13). Notice the Histogram in the original image shows a lack of tonal information in the highlights. In the corrected image, the tonal information is distributed across the entire Histogram. Also, you should bear in mind if you're looking at a printed copy of this book, the tonal difference may not be as obvious as it is on your computer monitor.

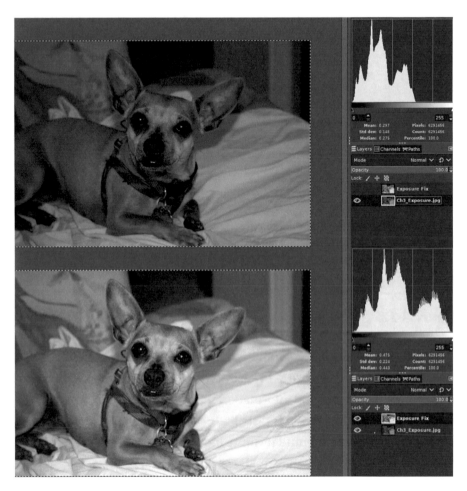

Figure 3-13. *The before-and-after comparison*

The Shadows-Highlights Dialog

This dialog is a little more complex than some of the other tonal adjustment dialogs. It's used to precisely control exposure in dark and light areas in the image.

Figure 3-14 shows the dialog and provides a brief description of the settings (except the bottom four, which should be self-explanatory):

1. *Presets*: Allows the user to pick from a preset list, save the current values settings as a preset, and manage presets.

2. *Shadows*: Adjusts the exposure in the shadow (darker) areas of the image.

3. *Shadows color adjustment*: Adjusts the saturation of shadows.

4. *Highlights*: Adjusts the exposure in the highlights (lighter) areas of the image.

5. *Highlights color adjustment*: Adjusts the saturation of highlights.

6. *White point adjustment*: Shift white point.

7. *Radius*: Spatial extent.

8. *Compress*: Compress the effect on shadow/ highlights and preserve the midtones.

9. *Blending Options*: Select from a list of blending modes; you can also adjust the opacity of the blend mode.

10. *Split view*: Provides a split before and after view before the action is committed.

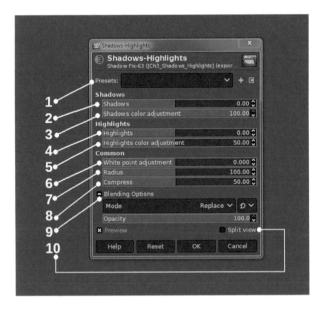

Figure 3-14. *The Shadows-Highlights dialog*

Tutorial 2: Using the Exposure Dialog

In this exercise, we'll use the Shadows-Highlights dialog to help bring out some detail in an image with harsh shadows (Figure 3-15).

Figure 3-15. *An image with harsh shadows*

To correct this image, follow these steps:

1. Open the image (*Ch3_shadows_highlights*) found in the Practice Images folder.

2. Duplicate the background layer (Shift + Control + D) and rename it Shadow Adjustment.

3. Move the *Shadows* slider to 75 and the *Radius* slider to 130, then click OK (Figure 3-16).

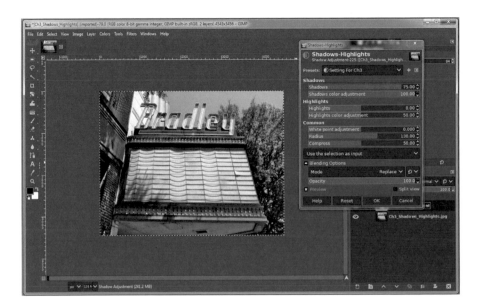

Figure 3-16. *Set the Shadows slider to 75 and the Radius slider to 130*

We can now see that the shadows are less harsh and reveal more image detail (Figure 3-17).

Figure 3-17. *The before-and-after comparison*

The Brightness-Contrast Dialog

This is a common tonal correction method that many beginners use. The Brightness-Contrast dialog (Figure 3-18) has two sliders: one for brightness and one for contrast. The adjustments are broad, with little ability to fine-tune, so this method of contrast adjustment has limits. When overused, it obliterates image detail.

Although it can be useful in some instances where a light adjustment is all that's required, the results can be destructive if you don't use it carefully. There are some images that just won't yield good results using this feature. Levels, curves, and layer blend modes are much better options.

Figure 3-18. *The Brightness and Contrast feature is a basic tonal correction tool*

Tutorial 3: Brightness-Contrast Adjustment

In this exercise, we're going to look at the basic Brightness-Contrast dialog. This image (Figure 3-19) is a bit flat and dull and can use an adjustment to make it "pop" a little more.

Figure 3-19. *The contrast is a bit dull in this image*

To correct this image, follow these steps:

1. Open the image (*Ch3_lincoln*) found in the Practice Images folder.

2. Duplicate the background layer (Shift + Control + D) and rename it Contrast Adjustment (Figure 3-20).

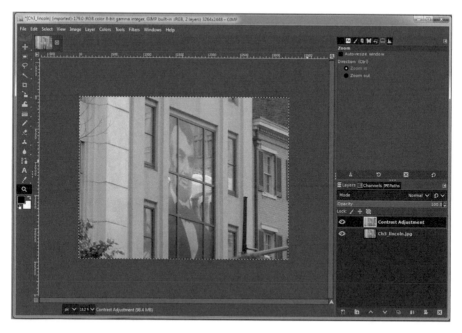

Figure 3-20. *The background layer duplicated and renamed Contrast Adjustment*

3. Open the Brightness-Contrast dialog (Image Menu ➤ Colors ➤ Brightness-Contrast).

4. Move the Brightness slider to 10 and the Contrast slider to 22, then click OK; this is a minor adjustment, but it makes a noticeable improvement (Figure 3-21).

Figure 3-21. *The contrast is now improved*

The Brightness-Contrast dialog can be useful for correcting images with minor tonal issues (Figure 3-22).

Figure 3-22. *The before-and-after comparison*

Tonal Corrections Using Levels

The Levels dialog allows you to shift the lightness values in the pixels to make tonal adjustments in the image you're working with. Essentially, this allows you to make an image lighter or darker or to change the contrast. It also lets you make color adjustments, which we'll look at in Chapter 4.

The Levels dialog displays a histogram, which is a graphical representation of the pixel values across the image, ranging from 0 (pure black) to 255 (pure white). Factors such as image tonality and exposure determine the shape of the histogram.

Figure 3-23 shows the dialog and provides a brief description of the settings (except the bottom four, which should be self-explanatory):

1. *Presets*: Allows the user to pick from a preset list, save the current values settings as a preset, and manage presets.

2. *Channel*: Adjusts the composite channel or the red, green, and blue channels individually.

3. *Input Levels*: The tonal information is essentially "remapped" by using the black, midtone, or white slider. The numeric input boxes can also be used. The eyedropper icons can also be used to pick black or white points to make a levels adjustment.

4. *Output Levels*: Allows the output level range to be limited or constrained; an example would be moving the white slider to the left, setting a lower maximum value for the highlights.

5. *Auto Input Levels*: Automatically adjusts the levels.

6. *Preview*: When this box is checked, the effect is shown in real time as the adjustments are being made.

7. *Adjust Levels Perceptually/Linear Histogram*: These are the default levels adjustment and histogram readout settings.

8. *Pick Black, Gray, or White Points for All Channels*: Makes tonal adjustments in the composite channel.

9. *Edit These Settings as Curves*: Instantly switches from the Levels to the Curves dialog.

10. *Split view*: Provides a split before and after view before the action is committed.

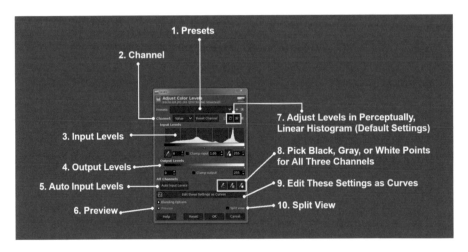

Figure 3-23. *The Levels dialog*

Tutorial 4: Correcting Contrast with Levels

In this exercise, we're going to improve the contrast in this image. As you can see in Figure 3-24, it has a flat tone, similar to the image in the previous tutorial. A simple levels adjustment will improve the contrast of this image and make it pop out more.

Figure 3-24. *An image with somewhat dull contrast*

To correct this image, follow these steps:

1. Open the image (*Ch3_bridge*) found in the Practice Images folder.

2. Duplicate the background layer (Shift + Control + D) and rename it Contrast Adjustment (Figure 3-25).

Figure 3-25. *The background layer duplicated and renamed*
Contrast Adjustment

3.   Open the Levels dialog box (Image Menu ➤ Colors
➤ Levels). Looking at the histogram, we can see that
the image pixels are mainly in the middle range; it
lacks shadow and highlight areas (Figure 3-26).

Figure 3-26. *The histogram shows the lack of the darkest and lightest pixels*

4. Take the following steps to adjust the contrast:

   - Move the black slider on the left toward the right and stop where the image data begins (the numeric value is about 54).

   - Repeat the same step with the white slider—move toward the left and stop where the image data begins (the numeric value is about 24.03).

   - Move the midpoint slider to the left until the numeric value is about 1.63, then click OK (Figure 3-27).

Figure 3-27. *Moving the black, white, and midpoint sliders as shown improves the contrast*

The image looks much better; the added contrast gives it more snap (Figure 3-28).

Figure 3-28. *The before-and-after comparison*

Tonal Corrections Using Curves

The Curves dialog allows you to make precise tonal edits. It's well worth investing the time and effort in learning to use this tool; it can help make tonal adjustments that other features either can't or won't do as well.

Figure 3-29 shows the dialog and provides a brief description of the settings (except the bottom four, which should be self-explanatory):

1. *Presets*: Allows the user to pick from a preset list, save the current values settings as a preset, and manage presets.

2. *Channel*: Adjusts the composite channel or the red, green, and blue channels individually.

3. *Curve*: This line can be curved to make adjustments in tone or color.

4. *Histogram*: Graphical display of pixel brightness.

5. *Input/Output*: Displays the x/y position of the cursor on the grid as the curve is being adjusted.

6. *Blending Options*: Select from a list of blending modes; you can also adjust the opacity of the blend mode.

7. *Preview*: When this box is checked, the effect is shown in real time as the adjustments are being made.

8. *Adjust Curves Perceptually/Linear Histogram*: These are the default levels adjustment and histogram readout settings.

9. *Curve type*: Choose either a smooth or freehand curve.

10. *Split view*: Provides a split before and after view before the action is committed.

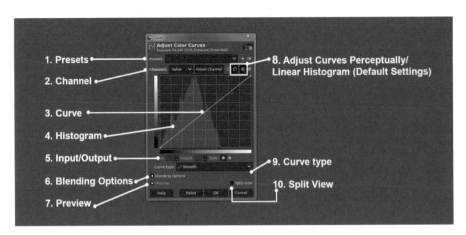

Figure 3-29. *The Curves dialog*

Tutorial 5: Correcting Contrast Using Curves

Another way to correct images with low contrast is to use the Curves dialog. We'll use this feature to make a slight S-shaped adjustment improve the contrast in the image shown (Figure 3-30).

Figure 3-30. *An image with less-than-optimal contrast*

To correct this image, follow these steps:

1. Open the image (*Ch3_cat*) found in the Practice Images folder.

2. Duplicate the background layer (Shift + Control + D). Rename the duplicate layer Contrast Adjustment (Figure 3-31).

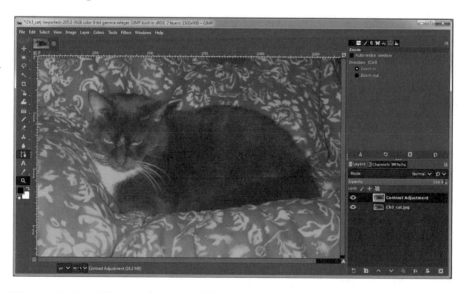

Figure 3-31. *The background layer duplicated and renamed Contrast Adjustment*

3. Open the Curves dialog (Colors ➤ Curves).

4. Now activate the Black Point layer, and open the Threshold dialog again. Move the black slider to the far left, then slowly toward the right, until the darkest cluster of pixels begins to emerge (Figure 3-32).

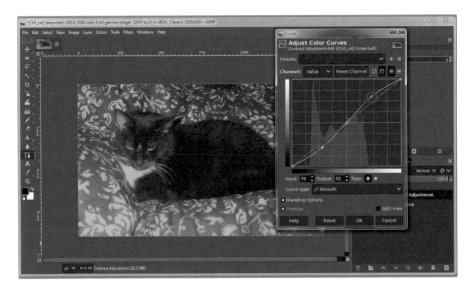

Figure 3-32. *Make a slight "S" curve to boost contrast*

The image now has better contrast and pops out more (Figure 3-33).

Figure 3-33. *The before-and-after comparison*

Tonal Corrections Using Layer Modes

Another method of correcting images with tonal problems is
experimenting with GIMP's *Layer Modes*, which are also referred to as
Blend Modes. Layer Modes alter the appearance of the image based on the
type of mode used. In this chapter, we'll only work with four different types
that can be useful for restoring images that are too light or dark.

I do recommend becoming acquainted with GIMP's Layer Modes—
they can be useful not only for image correction but for expanding
creativity as well. You can learn more about Layer Modes from the GIMP
User Manual: `https://docs.gimp.org/en/gimp-concepts-layer-`
`modes.html`.

Tutorial 6: Correcting Contrast in an Old Image

This is an old image from the 1950s that is a bit dull (Figure 3-34). Using
the *Soft Light* will boost the contrast quickly and easily.

Figure 3-34. *An old 1950s-era image in need of improved contrast*

To correct this image, follow these steps:

1. Open the image (*Ch3_1950s_holiday_image*) found in the Practice Images folder.

2. Duplicate the background layer (Shift + Control + D) and rename it Contrast Adjustment.

3. Change the layer's mode to Soft Light (Figure 3-35).

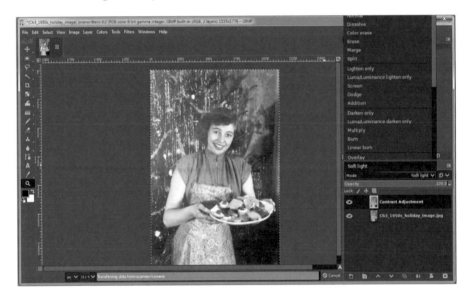

Figure 3-35. *Change the layer mode to Soft Light*

Note The Soft Light and Overlay modes essentially boost the contrast by making the shadows darker and the highlights lighter, as well as increasing saturation (color intensity). These methods of contrast adjustment can sometimes make the highlights too bright and shadows too dark, obscuring image detail.

4. Lower the layer's opacity to 90% to reduce the
    intensity of the highlights just a bit.

Using the Soft Light mode makes a noticeable boost in contrast, as we
can see in Figure 3-36.

Figure 3-36. *The before and after comparison*

Tutorial 7: Correcting a Dark Image

This image is quite dark due to underexposure (Figure 3-37).

Figure 3-37. *A dark, underexposed image*

To correct this image, follow these steps:

1. Open the image (*Ch3_dark_boat*) found in the Practice Images folder.

2. Duplicate the background layer (Shift + Control + D) and rename it Exposure Correction.

3. Change the layer mode to *Screen* (Figure 3-38); this lightens the image by lightening all pixels with a lightness value over 0 and under 255.

Figure 3-38. *The Screen layer mode lightens the image*

4. The image is greatly improved, but it still needs to
    be further lightened; duplicate the layer named
    Exposure Correction two times, and reduce the
    opacity of the top layer to 70% (Figure 3-39).

Figure 3-39. *Duplicate the layer named Exposure Correction two times, and reduce the top layer's opacity to 70%*

The image is now lightened and looks much better (Figure 3-40).

Figure 3-40. *The before-and-after comparison*

Tutorial 8: Correcting a Light, Faded Image

This exercise is similar to the previous one, except the goal is to darken an image that is too light (Figure 3-41).

Figure 3-41. *A faded, light image*

To correct this image, follow these steps:

1. Open the image (*Ch3_faded_photo*) found in the Practice Images folder.

2. Duplicate the background layer (Shift + Control + D) and rename it Exposure Correction.

3. Change the layer mode to *Multiply*; this will darken all pixels with a lightness value over 0 and under 255 (Figure 3-42).

Figure 3-42. *The Multiply layer mode darkens the image*

Figure 3-43 shows this faded image has been improved (note the color saturation in the sepia tone has been boosted as well).

Figure 3-43. *The before-and-after comparison*

Summary

In this chapter, you learned about the most common tonal problems and how they can be assessed using the histogram. The Color Picker tool is a useful tool for sampling pixels, to determine brightness and RGB values. The assortment of tutorials demonstrated some powerful methods for making a variety of tonal corrections in images using GIMP. In the next chapter, you'll learn about working with color.

CHAPTER 4

Color Correction and Restoration

In This Chapter

- Common Color Problems
- Color Essentials
- Correcting Color Casts
- Restoring Color
- Correcting Color Temperature

Common Color Problems

When color became mainstream, our family photographs took on a new dimension. While monochrome photographs possess an aura of mystery, color photographs have an element of added realism. When we look at an old color family photo in pristine condition, memories rush back more completely. We can instantly see the colors in a birthday cake or Halloween costume and relive those moments. Of course, it's distracting to view a cherished photograph that has faded or shifted colors.

© Phillip Whitt 2023
P. Whitt, *Beginning Photo Retouching and Restoration Using GIMP*,
https://doi.org/10.1007/978-1-4842-9265-5_4

There are several factors that can result in color problems: bad processing, the wrong film type or camera settings, chemical changes over time, etc. The following are the color problems that often plague images:

- Color casts and color shifts

- Faded color and extreme color loss

For me, one of the most challenging aspects I encounter as a professional retoucher is restoring images that have suffered extreme color loss, owing to fading over time. Many of these images were displayed in frames and exposed to damaging UV light that caused fading and color shifts. Many of the photographic papers and chemicals used during the late 1960s through the 1980s resulted in unstable prints that degraded at an accelerated rate.

Tip   I recommend downloading the free PDF version of the book *The Permanence and Care of Color Photographs: Traditional and Digital Color Prints, Color Negatives, Slides, and Motion Pictures* by Henry Wilhelm (Preservation Pub. Co., 1993). It's available from `www.wilhelm-research.com` and contains a wealth of information about the stability and longevity of various makes and types of photographic materials.

Color Essentials

Before moving on to the tutorials, there are a few essentials that must be covered. In this section, you'll learn about *additive* and *subtractive* color models and using the Color Picker tool to sample and determine color values. We'll also look briefly at the RGB *color channels*.

Additive Color

The color we see on a computer monitor is composed of light, which is *additive color*. The most commonly use color model is RGB (which stands for red, green, and blue light). This is the default mode for working with images in GIMP. The RGB color mode can produce a little over 16.7 million colors. Full intensity of red, green, and blue light results in white (Figure 4-1), while zero intensity of each results in black. When the percentages of each are equal, it produces a shade of gray between black and white (as we saw in Chapter 3), but when the percentages differ, the result is a colorized hue.

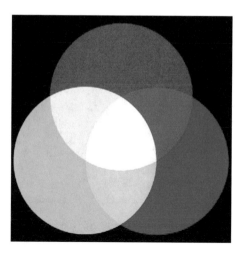

Figure 4-1. *The RGB (additive) color model*

Subtractive Color

Subtractive color is based on the absorption and reflection of light from printed pigments, dyes, and inks. Colors that are absorbed by a particular ink, pigment, or dye are being subtracted. For example, red ink reflects a red wavelength of light, but all other color wavelengths are absorbed. Black ink absorbs all color wavelengths, resulting in an absence of any color.

The CMYK color model is widely used in the offset printing industry. *CMYK* refers to the ink colors cyan, magenta, yellow, and black (the *K* is assigned to black, because it means "key" in the printing industry). Theoretically, equal combinations of cyan, magenta, and yellow ink produce black (Figure 4-2), but in actual practice, the result is a dark brown. This necessitates black as a fourth color, for accurate reproduction of grays and black in print.

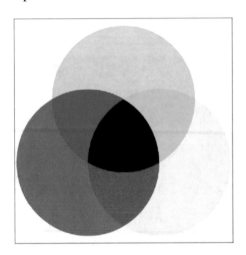

Figure 4-2. *The CMYK (subtractive) color model*

The RGB color model displays a much wider color range, or *gamut,* than the CMYK model. That's why an image displayed on your monitor often appears to be more vivid than the printed version.

Tip   For creating a color-managed work environment, you might want to invest in color measurement devices known as colorimeters and spectrophotometers. These devices come with their own configuration software.

The Color Picker Tool

In the previous chapter, we used this tool to evaluate tone in a grayscale image. It's a good idea to develop the habit of using this tool for sampling and evaluating color values in the images you edit. Even if you have a well-calibrated monitor, the Color Picker tool will show you the actual color values you are working with.

In Figure 4-3, we can see the shoes are reddish in color, but sampling the area indicated shows the exact percentages of red, green, and blue under the RGB setting (make sure the Use Info Window option is checked). This tool will sample single pixels or an average of surrounding pixels, depending on the Radius setting used. In addition to the default RGB setting, it also displays readouts in the HSV (hue, saturation, value) and the CMYK modes.

Note   The Color Picker tool in GIMP isn't currently color-managed, so the CMYK value should be viewed as an approximation of the color when printed.

The Color Picker tool is useful for identifying color casts in images, as we'll see a little later in this chapter.

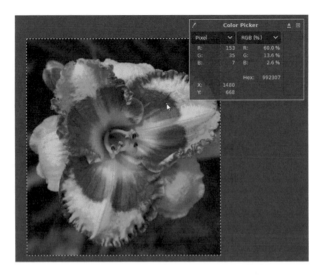

Figure 4-3. *Sampling an area using the Color Picker tool*

Color Channels

An RGB color image is a composite of three "storage bins," or channels of color data, one of each for red, green, and blue. Note where each color is represented by the brighter areas in each color channel (Figure 4-4).

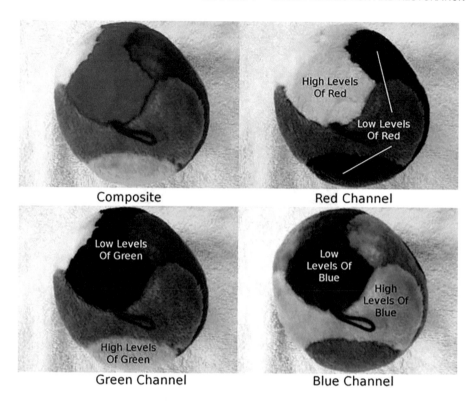

Figure 4-4. *Color channels store color data for an RGB image*

In GIMP, the channels are accessed in the Channels Palette. The tab to access the palette is right next to the Layers Palette tab (Figure 4-5). In some types of restoration work, it will be necessary to make adjustments to a specific color channel. The last tutorial in this chapter involves making an edit to a specific channel in a fairly complex color-correction exercise. Later in this book, we'll also look at how some restorations can be done by merely keeping one channel and discarding the others.

Figure 4-5. *The Channels Palette*

Correcting Color Casts

A color cast is a predominance of a certain color throughout the entire image. Color casts are usually unwanted, but sometimes, a photographer might be attempting a certain artistic effect for which the color cast is desirable. Most of the time, however, they are just a representative of pictures that have gone wrong. Color casts can be the result of a number of factors: the wrong film type used for the light source, incorrect white balance setting in digital cameras, etc.

The Color Balance feature (Colors ➤ Color Balance) in GIMP essentially offsets a color cast by increasing its opposite color. In the example shown in Figure 4-6, the Color Balance dialog is used to remove the blue color cast by introducing more yellow (which is the opposite of blue on the color wheel) and a slight amount of red to offset the cyan.

Figure 4-6. *The Color Balance dialog offsets the color cast by introducing more of the opposite color*

While the Color Balance dialog can be useful for minor color corrections, most will require more advanced methods (such as Levels or Curves).

Tutorial 9: Color Correction Using Auto Input Levels

This photo (Figure 4-7) was taken in the early 1960s and has undergone a color shift over the years. In this lesson, we'll use the *Auto Input Levels* feature, plus a manual Levels adjustment to make a quick and easy correction. This function essentially remaps the tonal information within each color channel, resulting in an improved image. This feature is hit-or-miss; sometimes, it works well, and sometimes the image will require more finesse (which we'll see a little later in this chapter).

Figure 4-7. *An image with a color cast*

To correct this image, follow these steps:

1. Open the image (*Ch4_auto_levels_input*) found in the Practice Images folder.

2. Duplicate the background layer (Shift + Control + D) and rename it Color Correction (Figure 4-8).

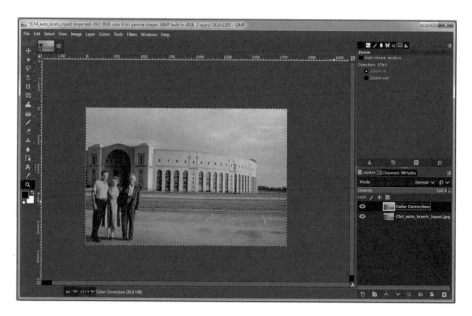

Figure 4-8. *Rename the duplicate layer Color Correction*

3.   We can see by merely looking at the image that it has
a red color cast, but because I'd like to encourage
you to get in the habit of using the Color Picker
tool, we'll take a reading. Open the Color Picker
tool (keyboard shortcut O). Sample from a neutral
color area, such as the concrete curb. The readout
shows a higher percentage of red than green or blue
(Figure 4-9).

Figure 4-9. *Taking a color sample from the concrete curb*

4. Open the Levels dialog (Colors ➤ Levels).

5. Click the Auto Input Levels button, but do not click
    the OK button just yet (Figure 4-10); the image
    colors will instantly look much better.

Figure 4-10. *The Auto Input Levels instantly color-corrects this image*

6.   The adjustment caused the white clouds to "blow
     out" some, meaning a loss of some detail; to correct
     this, move the *Output Levels* slider to 245, then click
     OK (Figure 4-11). This causes a slight loss in shadow
     areas, so it's important not to overuse the Output
     Levels slider.

Figure 4-11. *Move the Output Levels slider to 245, then click OK*

7. Open the Color Picker tool (keyboard shortcut O)
    and take another reading along the concrete curb
    (Figure 4-12); there is now only slightly more red
    than green and blue, so it appears more gray.

Figure 4-12. *Use the Color Picker tool to sample the gray hue in the concrete curb*

The end result looks much better (Figure 4-13).

Figure 4-13. *The before and after comparison*

Tutorial 10: Correcting a Severe Color Shift

This image, taken in the 1950s (Figure 4-14), has what can be safely described as a severe color cast.

For correcting this photo, we'll once again use the Auto Input Levels feature (this will help rebalance the colors). Because of the severity of the color shift, we'll need to make some additional edits using the Hue-Saturation dialog.

Figure 4-14. *An image with a strong red color cast*

To correct this image, follow these steps:

1. Open the image (*Ch4_severe_color_shift*) found in the Practice Images folder.

2. Duplicate the background layer and rename it Color Correction (Figure 4-15).

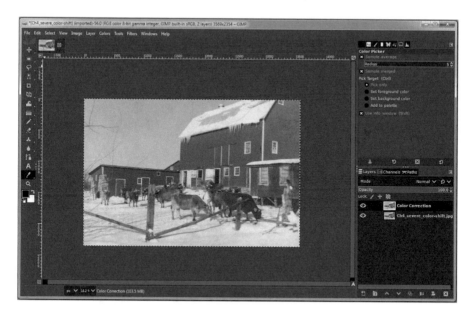

Figure 4-15. *Color correction edits will be made on a duplicate layer*

3. We'll now identify the color cast (it might be obvious, but let's double-check anyway). Open the Color Picker tool (O) and sample the area shown in Figure 4-16.

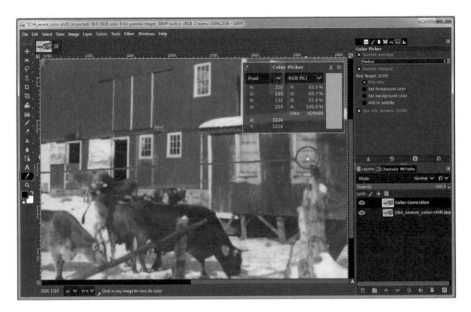

Figure 4-16. *Taking a color sample from the most color-neutral part of the image*

4. Open the Levels dialog box (Colors ➤ Levels).

5. Click the Auto Input Levels button, then click OK; the image is noticeably improved, but needs a little more work to help the colors look more natural (Figure 4-17).

Figure 4-17. *The auto feature produced good results*

6. Open the Hue/Saturation dialog (Colors ➤
    Hue-Saturation).

7. As shown in Figure 4-18, move the *Hue* slider to the
    right until it reads 70.00, move the *Saturation* slider
    to the right until it reads 90.00, then click OK.

Figure 4-18. *Move the Hue slider until it reads 70.00, move the Saturation slider until it reads 90.00, then click OK*

As we can see in the before-and-after comparison, the red cast has been eliminated, and the image looks much better (Figure 4-19).

Figure 4-19. *The before-and-after comparison*

Tutorial 11: Color Correction Using Levels (No. 1)

In this lesson, we'll use the *Pick gray point for all channels* feature in the Levels dialog to correct the mild purple/magenta color cast in the image shown (Figure 4-20), which was taken in the early 1990s. This color cast most likely resulted from faulty processing by the photo lab that processed the print, or the chemicals used during the processing may have been at fault.

Figure 4-20. *This photo has a color cast probably due to faulty processing or chemicals*

1. Open the image (*Ch4_RV*) found in the Practice Images folder.

2. Duplicate the background layer (Shift + Control + D) and rename it Color Correction.

3. Open the Color Picker tool (O).

4. Sampling the side of the RV indicates that blue is
    the prevalent color, followed by red, resulting in the
    purple color cast (Figure 4-21).

Figure 4-21. *The preponderance of blue, followed by red, results in a*
purple color cast

5. Open the Levels dialog (Colors ➤ Levels).

6. Using the *Pick gray point for all channels* feature
    (represented by an eyedropper icon with a gray
    square next to it), click in the area shown in
    Figure 4-22.

Figure 4-22. *Select the Pick gray point eyedropper icon and click in the area shown, then click OK*

We can now see the purple color cast is gone (Figure 4-23). This method of color correction is very useful for quick edits, but it may not always yield optimum results. It's possible to achieve even better results when using the Levels dialog to make manual, precise adjustments as we'll see in the lesson.

Figure 4-23. *The before-and-after comparison*

Tutorial 12: Color Correction Using Levels (No. 2)

In this lesson, we'll work with another image with a severe red color shift—so much so, we don't really need to use the Color Picker tool in this lesson (Figure 4-24). This time, we'll use the Levels dialog to make adjustments in each color channel to rebalance the colors.

Note   In Chapter 3, the tonal adjustments made on the grayscale images with Levels used the default Value setting in the dialog box. Grayscale images only have one gray channel. In RGB color images, the Value setting is a composite of the tonal information in the red, green, and blue color channels. Adjusting Levels using the Value setting makes broad color changes in the image, whereas adjusting each color channel is more precise.

Figure 4-24. *This image has a severe red color shift*

1. Open the image (*Ch4_ladies_on_patio*) found in the Practice Images folder.

2. Duplicate the background layer and rename it Color Correction.

3. Open the Levels dialog box (Colors ➤ Levels).

4. Select the Red color channel, then move the black point slider to the right until the numeric value reads 125; move the white point slider to the left until the numeric value reads 232 (Figure 4-25). *Do not click the OK button just yet.*

Figure 4-25. *Adjusting the levels in the Red channel*

5. Select the Green color channel, then move the Black
    Point slider to the right until the numeric value
    reads 10; move the White Point slider to the left until
    the numeric value reads 212 (Figure 4-26). *Do not
    click the OK button just yet.*

Figure 4-26. *Adjusting the levels in the Green channel*

6. Select the Blue color channel, then move the Black
    Point slider to the right until the numeric value
    reads 50; move the White Point slider to the left until
    the numeric value reads 214 (Figure 4-27). *Click the
    OK button now to commit the change.*

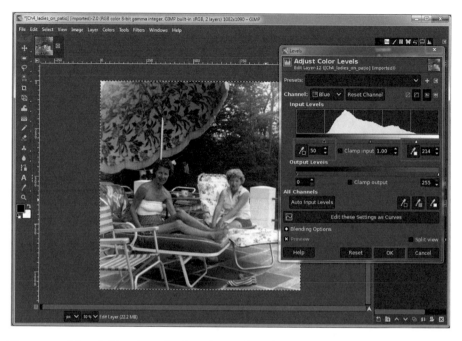

Figure 4-27. *Adjusting the levels in the Blue channel*

7. Now, we'll make some minor adjustments using the *Dodge/Burn* tool; activate this tool (Shift + D).

8. Make sure the Burn setting is ticked, and select Midtones; set the opacity to about 30%.

9. Using a large, soft brush, darken the corners slightly as shown in Figure 4-28.

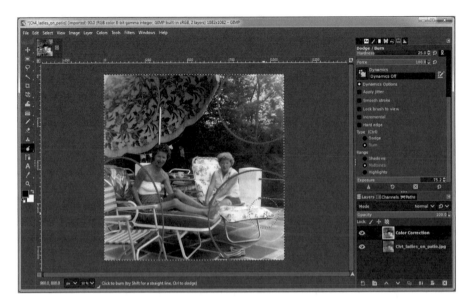

Figure 4-28. *Use the Burn tool to darken the corners just slightly*

10. The last thing to do is to brighten the overall image just a bit; open the Levels dialog (Colors ➤ Levels).

11. Move the Midpoint slider slightly to the left until the numeric readout is 1.10, then click OK (Figure 4-29).

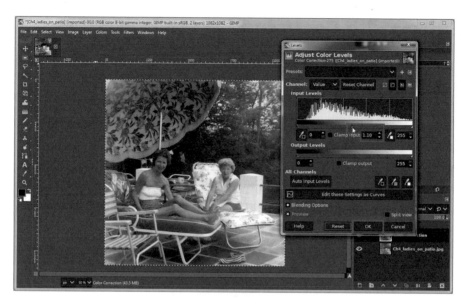

Figure 4-29. *Move the Midpoint slider until it reads 1.10*

Now, we can see that although not perfect, this image is vastly improved—especially considering how damaged the original was (Figure 4-30).

Figure 4-30. *The before-and-after comparison*

Tutorial 13: Restoring Severe Color Loss Using the Curves and Hue-Saturation Dialogs

The following image has lost a great deal of color information over the years. The photograph (Figure 4-31) was taken in 1966 and has suffered severely since then. This tutorial will be a little longer than usual. We'll use curves to do the majority of the corrections, but there will be some extra steps required to bring it back to (almost) new.

Figure 4-31. *An image from the mid-1960s with severe color loss*

To correct this image, follow these steps:

1. Open the image (*Ch4_little_boy*) found in the Practice Images folder.

2. Open the Crop tool (Shift + C) and trim the borders away from the image (Figure 4-32), so they don't "contaminate" the adjustment (as discussed in the Introduction).

3. Using the Rotate tool (Shift + R), move the image
    slightly counter-clockwise, to straighten it.

Figure 4-32. *Cropping the borders to achieve accurate curve*
adjustments

4. Duplicate the background layer and rename it Color
    Restore (Figure 4-33).

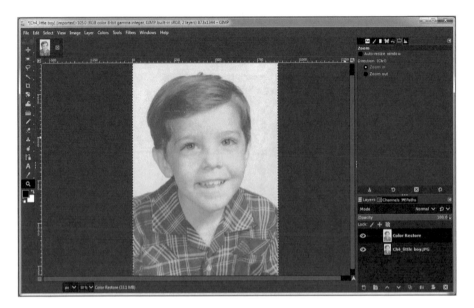

Figure 4-33. *Color correction edits will be made on a duplicate layer*

5. Open the Curves dialog box (Image Menu ➤ Colors
    ➤ Curves). As in the previous tutorial, because
    each color channel has a different tonal value, we're
    going to make adjustments on each one, to revive
    both contrast and color. In the Channels option,
    select the Red color channel (Figure 4-34). Move
    the node to the left, stopping where the image
    data begins. (Wait until you adjust all three color
    channels before clicking OK.)

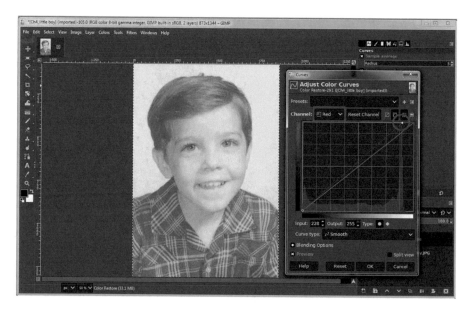

Figure 4-34. *Adjusting the Red channel in the Curves dialog*

6. Select the Green color channel and move the nodes
    to where the image information begins on the sides
    of the histogram (Figure 4-35).

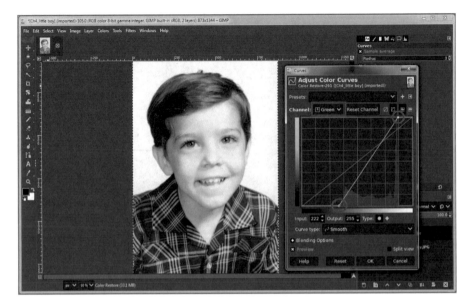

Figure 4-35. *Adjusting the Green channel in the Curves dialog*

7.   Select the Blue color channel and move the nodes
to where the image information begins on the sides
of the histogram (Figure 4-36). *Don't click OK just
yet.* We're going to make one more minor Curves
adjustment.

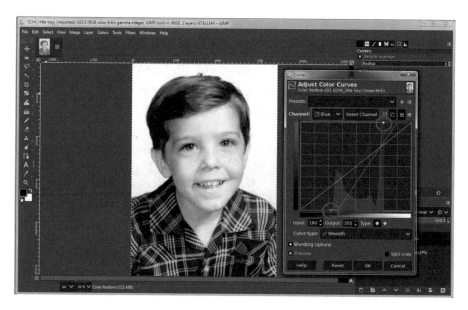

Figure 4-36. *Adjusting the Blue channel in the Curves dialog*

8. The image is now much better. The skin looks pale, so now we'll warm it up just a little. Click the Curves adjustment in the center and pull down just slightly (Figure 4-37). Now you can click OK.

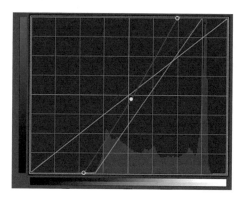

Figure 4-37. *This minor adjustment on the Blue channel warms the image slightly*

9. Now, open the Hue/Saturation dialog box (Image
    Menu ➤ Colors ➤ Curves). Adjust the Hue setting
    to –10 and boost the Saturation by 10. This will
    further improve the overall color balance and
    saturation (Figure 4-38).

Figure 4-38. *Making further improvements with Hue/Saturation*

10. We'll now replace some of the density that was lost
    over time. Duplicate the Color Restore layer and
    rename it Density Restore. Set the blend mode
    to Multiply and lower the opacity to about 30%
    (Figure 4-39). Merge the Density Restore layer down
    to the Color Restore layer.

Figure 4-39. *Improving density with the Multiply blend mode*

11. Duplicate the Color Restore layer again.

12. Open the Dodge/Burn tool (Shift + D). In the tool
     options, use the following settings:

     1. Burn

     2. Midtones

     3. Exposure –15%

Using a large, soft brush, darken the lips slightly on the Color Restore
layer copy (Figure 4-40). If you overdo it, you can lower the layer's opacity
to reduce the effect.

135

Figure 4-40. *Darkening the lips slightly with the Burn tool*

13. The darker areas in the hair have a green tinge, so we'll correct that now. Create a new layer and name it Hair. Change the blend mode to Color. Using the Color Picker tool, sample some brown from the hair, to change the active color.

14. Paint over the darker areas using a large, soft brush to paint over the green tinge with brown (Figure 4-41). Lower the layer's opacity some, if necessary.

Figure 4-41. *Removing the green tinge by painting brown over a layer set to the Color blend mode*

15. Create a new layer; set the blend mode to Color and the opacity to about 8%. Using red as the active color and a large, soft brush, paint over the cheeks and ears, to add a little natural coloring. It's a subtle but important touch (Figure 4-42).

Figure 4-42. *Adding a slight amount of red to the cheeks and ears*

The image is now looking more like it should (Figure 4-43). It's amazing how far along GIMP brought this image.

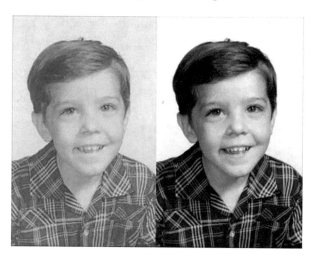

Figure 4-43. *The before-and-after comparison*

Tutorial 14: Correcting Color Temperature

Taking a photo using the improper color temperature setting can result in an image that looks too cool (or too warm in some cases). The image in Figure 4-44 is an example of an outdoor scene that's a bit too cool. In this lesson, we'll use the Color Temperature dialog to warm it up.

Figure 4-44. *This image has a cool color temperature; using the Color Temperature dialog will help warm it up*

1. Open the image (*Ch4_color_temp*) found in the Practice Images folder.

2. Duplicate the background layer (Shift + Control + D) and rename it Color Correction.

3. Open the Color Temperature dialog (Colors ➤ Color Temperature).

4. Click the small triangle to the right of the *Intended temperature* setting—the preset menu will open. Select 9300 K (the K represents Kelvin, the standard unit of measurement used for color temperature), then click OK (Figure 4-45).

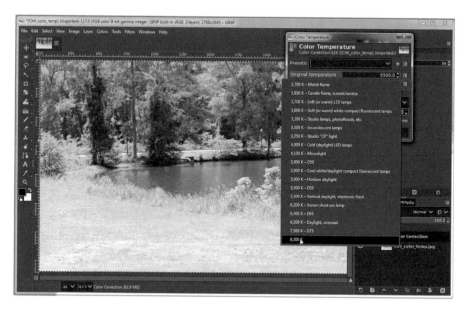

Figure 4-45. *Select the 9300 K present, then click OK*

We can now see that the image looks noticeably warmer (Figure 4-46).

Figure 4-46. *The before-and-after comparison*

Note   The Color Temperature dialog also has manual sliders to adjust the original and intended temperatures.

Summary

Color correction is a vital part of the photo retouching and restoration world. Being familiar with the additive and subtractive color models, color channels, and use of the Color Picker tool helps in making color corrections. Color casts are common in both old and newer photographic images, and GIMP has numerous options for correcting them.

GIMP is capable of restoring images with severe color loss, through such powerful features as Levels and Curves and layer blend modes, and by adjusting damaged color channels. In the next chapter, we'll look at ways to enhance images through the creative use of color, such as digital sepia toning and colorizing grayscale images.

CHAPTER 5

Creative Use of Color

In This Chapter

- Reimagine Your Pictures
- Converting Color into Black and White
- Digital Sepia Toning
- Selective Colorizing
- Colorizing Black-and-White Images

Reimagine Your Pictures

GIMP is the ideal program to reimagine your favorite images. Transport pictures back in time by converting them into black and white or sepia tone. You can give an old black-and-white portrait a new dimension by colorizing it. With GIMP and some imagination, you can be as creative as you want with the images you work with.

© Phillip Whitt 2023
P. Whitt, *Beginning Photo Retouching and Restoration Using GIMP*,
https://doi.org/10.1007/978-1-4842-9265-5_5

Converting Color into Black and White

The widespread availability of color photography certainly revolutionized the industry. I mentioned in the previous chapter how color opened up a new world to our photograph-viewing pleasure. However, black and white is still enjoyed by many. Some images you capture will just naturally seem to lend themselves to black and white—it's basically working with color in reverse (for lack of a better phrase).

It might seem that converting a color image into black and white is just a matter of draining the color away. You can simply use the Hue/Saturation dialog and reduce the color saturation to zero. While that does work in the sense that it removes color, it will often leave behind an image that is flat, dull, or even unnatural looking, depending on the colors in the original image.

Note   You've probably noticed that I've used the term *grayscale* in earlier chapters when referring to what are normally known as black-and-white images. Grayscale is technically the proper term to refer to a digital image that is made up of black, white, and shades of gray. In the world of photography, such an image is typically referred to as black and white, so for the purposes of this book, I use the terms interchangeably.

In Figure 5-1, the Hue-Saturation dialog was used to remove the color from the red flower. Using the *Lightness* slider brightens or darkens the image, so this dialog offers a limited degree of control when converting color images into black and white.

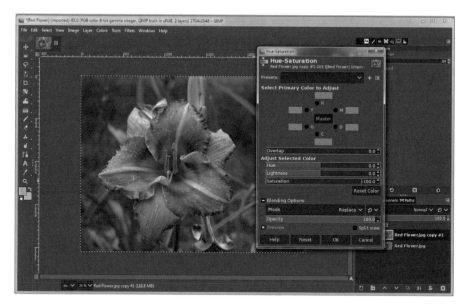

Figure 5-1. *Using the Hue-Saturation dialog offers a limited degree of control when converting color into black and white*

In some instances, the Hue-Saturation may work just fine, especially for making quick conversions. However, the next three tutorials will guide you in methods that offer more control to help you achieve the best results.

Tutorial 15: Converting Color to Black and White (No. 1)

The *Color to Gray* dialog (Colors ➤ Desaturate ➤ Color to Gray) offers more flexibility than using the Hue-Saturation dialog. With this option, you can control the effect by using the Radius, Samples, and Iterations sliders.

Here's a description of what each slider does (each description appears by hovering the cursor over the slider):

- *Radius*: Neighborhood taken into account, this is the radius in pixels taken into account when deciding which colors map to which gray values.

- *Samples*: Number of samples to do per iteration looking for the range of colors.

- *Iterations*: A higher number of iterations provide less noisy results at a computational cost.

Enabling the *Enhance Shadows* function boosts details in a shadow at the expense of noise.

We'll use the Color to Gray dialog to convert the image shown in Figure 5-2 into black and white.

Figure 5-2. *The Color to Gray dialog will be used to convert this image into black and white*

1. Open the image (*Ch5_serval*) found in the Practice Images folder.

2. Duplicate the background layer and rename it Edit Layer.

3. Open the Color to Gray dialog box (Colors ➤ Desaturate ➤ Color to Gray).

4. Set the Radius to 516, the Samples to 12, and the Iterations to 14; enable Enhance Shadows and click OK (Figure 5-3).

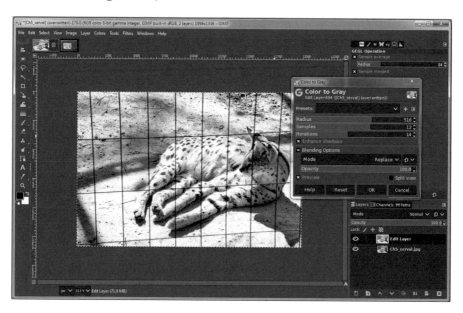

Figure 5-3. *Use the settings shown to convert this image to black and white*

Figure 5-4 shows the before and after comparison. The Color to Gray dialog is well worth experimenting with—one downside is that it may work slowly on older computers because of the resource requirements. However, it does provide a wide range of adjustment, so you can fine-tune the results.

Figure 5-4. *The before-and-after comparison*

Tutorial 16: Converting Color to Black and White (No. 2)

The *Desaturate* dialog uses *modes* based on Luminance, Luma, Lightness (HSL), Average (HSI Intensity), or Value (HSV). Basically, each mode uses a specific type of mathematical calculation to achieve shades of gray in the image (Figure 5-5).

Unlike the Color to Gray dialog, using one of these modes is a "one-shot" operation. You can try each mode out to determine which one works best on your image—once you click OK, the action is committed.

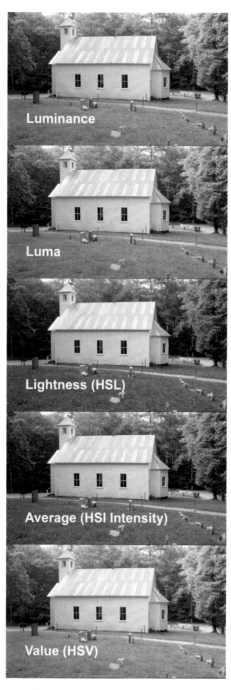

Figure 5-5. *The Desaturate dialog offers five modes*

To convert this image, follow these steps:

1. Open the image (*Ch5_old_church*) found in the Practice Images folder.

2. Duplicate the background layer and rename it Black and White Layer.

3. Open the Desaturate dialog box (Colors ➤ Desaturate ➤ Desaturate).

4. Click the Mode menu, and you can try each one out (for the purposes of this lesson, select Luminance, then click OK).

Determining which option to choose really depends on what looks best to you. As with many aspects of image editing, there is an element of subjectivity involved. Personally, I thought the Luminance setting looked the best, so I chose this option. It works very well for a quick conversion (Figure 5-6).

Figure 5-6. *The before and after comparison*

Tutorial 17: Converting Color to Black and White (No. 3)

Using the Mono Mixer (Figure 5-7) for converting color into black and white offers a greater degree of fine-tuning but takes some time and practice. It's worth the effort, so that you can end up with superb color to black-and-white conversions.

To convert this image, follow these steps:

1. Open the image (*Ch5_old_building*) found in the Practice Images folder.

2. Duplicate the background layer and rename it Black and White Layer.

3. Open the Mono Mixer dialog (Colors ➤ Desaturate ➤ Mono Mixer).

4. Use the following settings:

   • Red Channel Multiplier: 0.860

   • Green Channel Multiplier: 0.116

   • Blue Channel Multiplier: 0.058

   Click OK after settings are made.

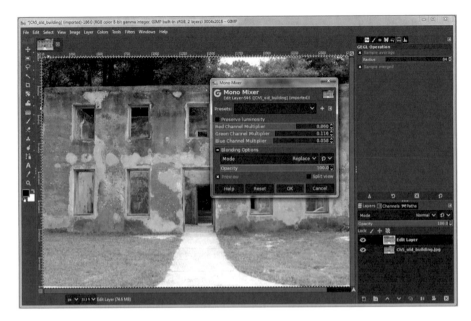

Figure 5-7. *Fine-tuning color to black-and-white conversions using the Mono Mixer*

This method is worth investing some time and practice. Using the "one-shot" methods of conversion may not always yield the results you want. In this case, we ended up with good contrast without compromising too much detail in the highlights or shadows.

Figure 5-8. *The before-and-after comparison*

Digital Sepia Toning

GIMP can effectively emulate the effect of sepia toning. In the traditional darkroom method, a chemical process is used on silver-based black-and-white photographic prints to give them a warm, brownish tone. Many photographs from the late 1800s and early 20th century are sepia toned. There are several ways to digitally apply a sepia tone using GIMP. We'll look at two in this chapter.

In the way that some images lend themselves to conversion from color to black and white, some can also be enhanced (or just given an artistic element) by applying a sepia tone. It works well with images such as the church we worked with previously. Like conversion to black and white, sepia toning seems to take an image back in time.

Tutorial 18: Converting Color to Sepia (No. 1)

We're going to work with the same image of the old building that was converted to black and white in the previous tutorial. This first method is a very easy and quick way to produce a sepia tone.

To convert this image, follow these steps:

1. Open the image (*Ch5_old_building*) found in the Practice Images folder.

2. Duplicate the background layer (Shift + Control + D) and rename it Sepia Layer.

3. Open the Sepia dialog (Colors ➤ Desaturate ➤ Sepia); set the *Effect Strength* to 100%, then click OK (Figure 5-9).

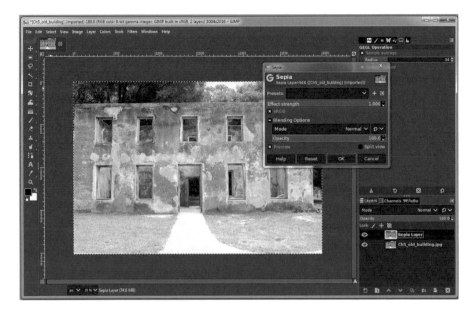

Figure 5-9. *Set the Effect Strength to 100% in the Sepia dialog*

Tutorial 19: Converting Color to Sepia (No. 2)

In this tutorial, we'll use a different approach to achieve a sepia tone. Although the method is different, the results are similar. I personally prefer this way of applying a sepia tone because it allows me to control the amount of sepia toning applied as well as the sepia hue.

To convert this image, follow these steps:

1. As in the previous lesson, open the image (*Ch5_old_building*) found in the Practice Images folder.

2. Duplicate the background layer (Shift + Control + D) and rename it Sepia Layer.

3. Open the *Colorize* dialog (Colors ➤ Colorize).

4. Set the *Hue* to approximately 0.0930, and the *Saturation* to approximately 0.4070, then click OK (Figure 5-10).

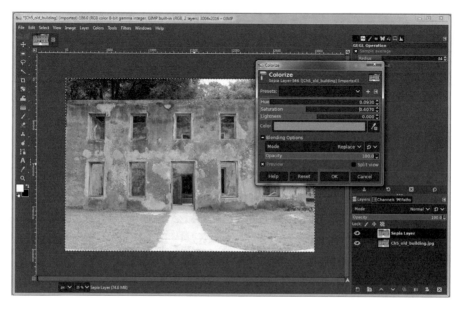

Figure 5-10. *Using the Colorize dialog to achieve a sepia tone*

You probably noticed that the hue is a bit more brown in this case as compared to the result using the Sepia dialog; sepia tones can vary somewhat, so this method of sepia toning offers more fine-tuning.

Figure 5-11 shows the before and after comparison.

Figure 5-11. *The before-and-after comparison*

Selective Colorizing

If you've ever seen the 1998 movie *Pleasantville*, then selective colorizing will probably seem familiar. In the movie, a teenage boy and his twin sister are transported into a fictional 1950s black-and-white sitcom. As the movie progresses, color begins to emerge here and there, mixed with a world made up of shades of gray. You can create some interesting images using this technique. I like to use it sparingly, by accenting a black-and-white image with small splashes of color. It's a fun technique to experiment with. Give it a try, using your own images.

Tutorial 20: Mixing Color with Black and White

This is the image that was converted into black and white earlier. It is also a good subject for selective colorizing (Figure 5-12).

Figure 5-12. *A good image for mixing color and black and white*

To convert this image, follow these steps:

1. Open the image (*Ch5_selective_color*) found
   in the Practice Images folder. This is a .PSD
   (Photoshop) file with two layers.

Note   I chose to use a .PSD format in case there are some readers
who might be using Adobe Photoshop instead of GIMP for these
tutorials. GIMP is perfectly capable of handling these files.

---

2. Right-click the Black and White Layer and add a
    layer mask from the drop-down menu (Figure 5-13).

Figure 5-13. *A layer mask added to the Black and White Layer*

3. Choose a soft brush with black as the active color
    and paint on the flowers, the girl's hair bow, etc., to
    reveal color from the layer beneath (Figure 5-14).

Figure 5-14. *Paint in the layer mask as shown to reveal the colors*

You can do more than what is shown, if you'd like to play around. If you don't like your results, switch to white and add the gray back to the areas where you don't want any color (Figure 5-15).

Figure 5-15. *The before and after comparison*

Tutorial 21: Mixing Color with Sepia

In this tutorial, we'll be mixing color with sepia. In this instance, the colors will be more muted, giving the image a unique look. Figure 5-16 shows the image we will be converting.

Figure 5-16. *The original image to convert to a sepia/color mix*

To edit this image, follow these steps:

1. Open the image (*Ch5_old_church_2*) found in the Practice Images folder.

2. Duplicate the background layer (Shift + Control + D) and rename it Sepia Layer.

3. Open the Colorize dialog box (Colors ➤ Colorize), set the Hue slider to a value of about 0.0750 and the Saturation to about 0.3500 (Figure 5-17), and click OK.

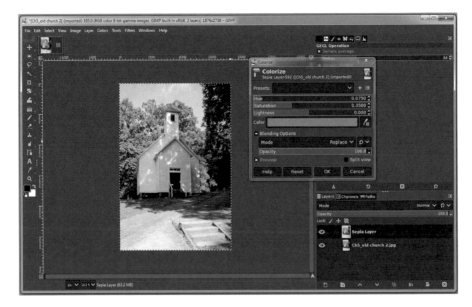

Figure 5-17. *Using the Colorize dialog to apply a sepia tone to the image*

4. Add a layer mask to the Sepia Layer (right-click Layer ➤ Add Layer Mask).

5. Activate the background layer by clicking it. Choose the Select by Color tool (Shift + O). Check the Feather Edges option and set the Radius to 10 pixels. Set the Threshold to 25.

6. Click inside the sky area (Figure 5-18).

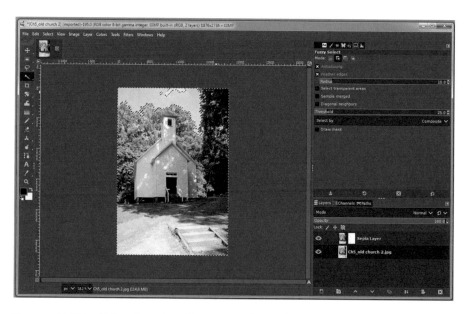

Figure 5-18. *Selecting the sky using the Select by Color tool*

7. For parts of the sky that weren't selected, choose
    the Free Select tool (F) and add to the selection by
    holding the Shift key and drawing around those
    areas (Figure 5-19). For areas that were selected but
    shouldn't have been, hold the Control key and draw
    around those areas to subtract them.

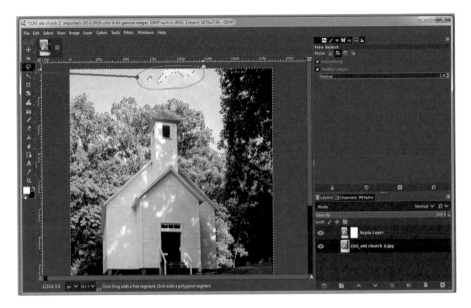

Figure 5-19. *Using the Free Select tool to add to the selection*

8. Click the layer mask to activate it. Double-click
    the foreground color swatch and set it to about
    25% gray.

9. Using the Bucket Fill tool (Shift + B), fill in the
    selected area to reveal some of the blue in the sky
    (Figure 5-20).

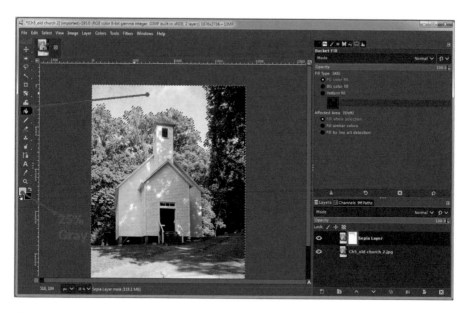

Figure 5-20. *By filling the selection with 25% gray in the active layer mask, only some of the color is revealed*

10. Choose a soft brush and paint in the image with various shades of lighter to middle range grays, revealing subtle colors throughout the image (Figure 5-21).

Figure 5-21. *Painting with various grays with the layer mask active to reveal subtle colors*

The end result is an image with a quaint, vintage look (Figure 5-22). You can vary the results by painting on the layer mask with black (which will reveal full color), various grays, and white (which will completely mask the colors).

Figure 5-22. *The before and after comparison*

Colorizing Black-and-White Images

I must admit this is one of my favorite editing activities. It's almost like working on a grown-up version of a coloring book—but with much better results. Adding color to old black-and-white images is requested by my clients fairly often, so it's a good skill to acquire for those offering their services professionally.

Tutorial 22: Colorizing Black-and-White Images

In this tutorial, we'll colorize an old family photo from the mid-1950s (Figure 5-23).

In this lesson, I'll provide the skin and hair values. The rest you can approximate, if you like. You don't have to match the clothing, wall, or table covering exactly. You can use the Hue/Saturation dialog (Image Menu ➤ Colors ➤ Hue/Saturation) on any layer you colorize to change the hue.

Figure 5-23. *A 1950s image perfect for colorizing*

To colorize this image, follow these steps:

1. Open the image (*Ch5_colorize_little_boy*) found in the Practice Images folder.

2. Duplicate the background (Shift + Control + D) and rename it Edit Layer.

3. Create a new layer (Shift + Control + N) and name it Skin (or Skin Tone). Change the layer's blend mode to HSL Color.

4. Using the Change Foreground Color dialog, pick a flesh color. You can double-click the foreground color swatch and input the values R 96.8, G 79.2, and B 60.1 in the Change Foreground dialog (Figure 5-24).

Figure 5-24. *The values to enter for flesh color*

5. Lower the Skin Layer's opacity to 30%–35% and paint in the flesh color, using a soft brush (Figure 5-25). You'll have to vary the brush size as you work, enlarging it to cover large areas and reducing it to paint small areas.

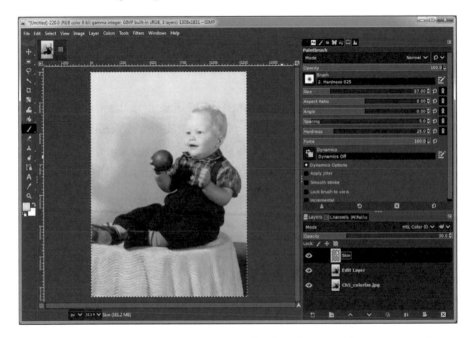

Figure 5-25. *Painting a translucent flesh color on a layer set to the HSL Color blend mode*

6. Add a layer mask to the Skin Layer (right-click Layer ➤ Add Layer Mask). Using a small, soft brush and a middle gray (50%) as the active color, paint on the layer mask to remove some of the skin color from the eyes (Figure 5-26).

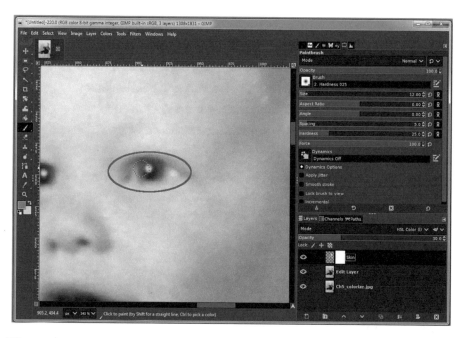

Figure 5-26. *Removing some of the color by painting on a layer mask*

7. Create a new layer (Shift + Control + N) and name it Hair. Change the layer's blend mode to Color.

8. Using the Change Foreground Color dialog, pick a pale yellow to use for a very light blond. The values used here are R 254, G 229, and B 162, which can be entered in the Change Foreground Color dialog.

9. Lower the Hair Layer's opacity to about 20%, and paint the blond color in, using a soft brush. You'll have to vary the size of the brush as you work, enlarging it to cover large areas and reducing it to paint small areas.

10. Repeat this process with the overalls, ball, socks, shoes, etc. All the layers will be set to the HSL Color blend mode, with the opacity varying from 30% to 35%. You'll have to experiment some to get the look you want (Figure 5-27). Add layer masks to your layers if you have to remove any excess color from around the edges.

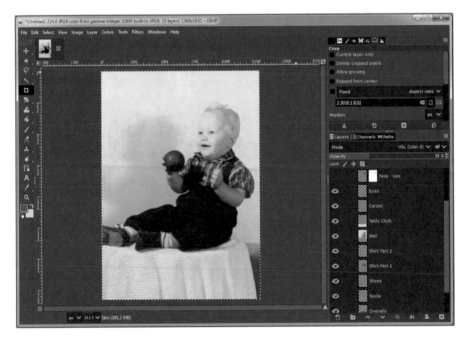

Figure 5-27. Adding color on layers set to the HSL Color blend mode

11. The finishing touches will be the eyes and the face. Create a new layer (Shift + Control + N) and set the blend mode to Color. Paint a little light blue to color the eyes. Don't overdo it, so that it will look natural. The layer opacity should be about 15%.

12. Last, create a new layer (Shift + Control + N) and set
the blend mode to Color. Paint some red on the lips,
cheeks, and ear. This layer will require low opacity—
about 9%–10%. Even set that low, I added a layer mask
(right-click Layer ➤ Add Layer Mask) and painted
away some of the excess red from the cheeks, using a
mid-gray as the color. You want just a *hint* of red, for a
look as close to natural as possible (Figure 5-28).

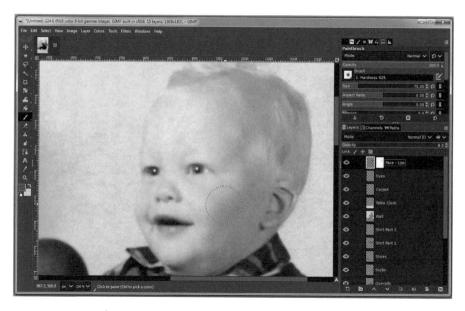

Figure 5-28. *Finishing with a hint of red in the cheeks*

Your version may look a little different from this one. It's OK to choose
different colors for the wall, tablecloth, etc. The main thing is making the
eyes, skin, lips, and hair look as natural as possible. For the wall and table
covering, I chose colors that looked like they would fit the time period, but
they can be varied.

One thing to remember when colorizing images is that it's better
to have colors that are a little undersaturated than too saturated.
Oversaturation doesn't look natural. That's why it's important to use a

separate layer for everything you colorize. You want to be able to fine-tune color intensity by adjusting layer opacity. With practice, you can achieve results that look reasonably realistic (Figure 5-29).

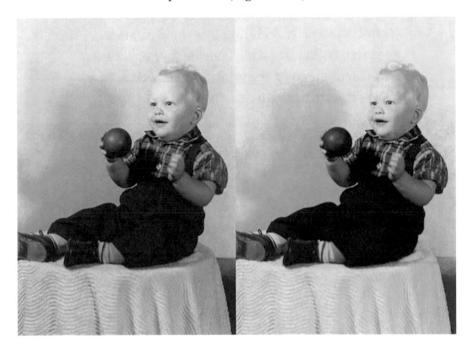

Figure 5-29. *The before and after comparison*

Summary

By using GIMP, you can get creative in the use of color in your images. Converting color images into black and white (I suppose one could argue) is still working with color—albeit in a backward kind of way. Adding a sepia tone to your images can give them a vintage look, and combining color with black and white or sepia introduces a unique, artistic look to images.

Colorizing black-and-white images can be really fun. Clients often request this service, so it pays to be skilled in colorizing images.

PART III

Digital Cleanup and Repairing Damage

CHAPTER 6

Dust, Light Scratch, and Stain Removal

In This Chapter

- Digital Cleanup with GIMP
- Removing Dust and Crud from Images

Digital Cleanup with GIMP

Many of the images you'll work with will require digital cleanup and repair. GIMP is the perfect tool for removing dust from scanned slides (i.e., the embedded dust that won't come off when doing the prescan cleaning we covered in Chapter 2). Using GIMP, you'll be able to remove unsightly small spots and scratches as well.

© Phillip Whitt 2023
P. Whitt, *Beginning Photo Retouching and Restoration Using GIMP*,
https://doi.org/10.1007/978-1-4842-9265-5_6

Removing Dust and Crud from Images

Older prints and slides often have embedded dust, small particles of dirt, etc., that will have to be digitally removed after scanning. Transparencies, in particular, are often plagued with dust, dirt, and mold particles. While some scanners have built-in "dust removal" features in their software, these can often soften the image a great deal in the process. Using the tools GIMP has to offer will allow a more precise, surgical approach to removing imperfections, thus maintaining the overall sharpness of the image. The tutorials in this chapter will give you some useful practice for eventually tackling heavy damage, as we'll see in the next chapter.

Tutorial 23: Removing Dust from a Slide

This slide from the 1950s (Figure 6-1) has a great deal of dust particles embedded throughout, but this is most noticeable in the sky area. Dust removal can be a time-consuming task, but in some instances, it can be sped up. The dust in the sky area can be almost completely obliterated in a couple of minutes.

Figure 6-1. *An image with a great deal of embedded dust (Image courtesy of the Bundt family)*

To correct this image, follow these steps:

1. Open the image (*Ch6_dust_busting*) found in the Practice Images folder.

2. Duplicate the background layer (Shift + Control + D) and rename it Dust Clean Up Layer.

3. Open the Free Select tool (F) and set the Feather Edges radius to 10 pixels (Figure 6-2).

Figure 6-2. Use the Free Select tool to make a selection around the sky

4. We'll now copy this selection and paste it as a new layer (Control + C and Control + V). It will appear as a floating selection in the Layers palette. Right-click the floating selection and select the To New Layer option from the drop-down menu.

5. Rename the layer Sky and change the blend mode to Lighten only (Figure 6-3).

Figure 6-3. *Changing the blend mode to Lighten only*

6. Select the Move tool (M) and click in the sky area
    (Figure 6-4). Using the left arrow key, nudge the
    layer a few times to the right and up a couple of
    times until most of the dust vanishes (the Lighten
    only blend mode lightens the dark dust specks).

Figure 6-4. Nudging the layer slightly to remove the dust

7. Repeat the process of selecting other areas with large areas of dark dust specks, such as the tile (Figure 6-5), and copying the selected areas to new layers set to the Lighten only blend mode.

Figure 6-5. *Repeating the dust removal process in the tile area*

8. There will be some dust that will have to be removed manually, using the Healing and Clone tools. Use the Dust Removal Layer to do the cleanup work (Figure 6-6).

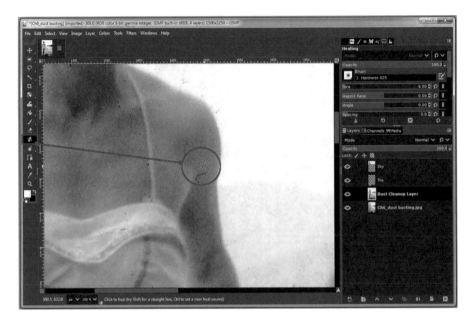

Figure 6-6. *Cleaning up the remaining dust with the Healing and Clone tools*

This method of dust removal greatly reduces the amount of time required for repair (Figure 6-7). This can be extremely useful when cleaning up batches of slides or negatives.

Figure 6-7. *The before and after comparison*

Note   This method of mass dust removal, which we performed on the sky portion of the image, should be used on areas of unimportant image detail, such as the sky and clouds, solid walls (with no patterns), concrete sidewalks, etc.

Tutorial 24: Removing Dust and Light Scratches

We corrected the color in this image back in Chapter 4 (Figure 6-8), and now it's time to clean up the light scratches, blemishes, and dust.

Figure 6-8. *Image requiring light cleanup*

To correct this image, follow these steps:

1. Open the image (*Ch6_light_clean_up*) found in the Practice Images folder.

2. Duplicate the background layer (Shift + Control + D) and rename it Heal-Clone Layer (Figure 6-9). These are the two tools we'll be using for most of the editing on this image.

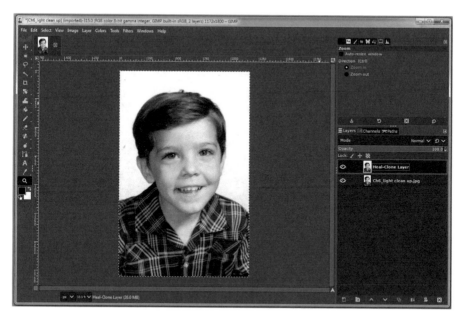

Figure 6-9. *The Heal-Clone Layer, where most of the editing will be done*

3. We'll start with the scratch above the eye. Activate the Healing tool (H). Choose the brush with the 050 hardness value from the tool options. Set the brush size to just slightly larger than the scratch.

4. Click an area nearby to sample the tone and texture and drag along the scratch to remove it. Resample frequently as you work (Figure 6-10).

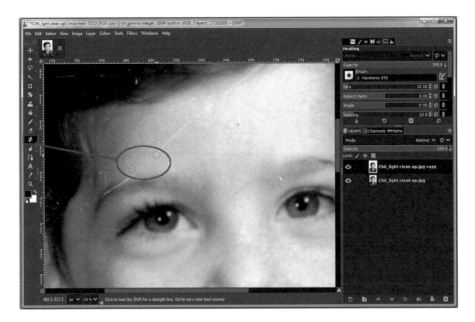

Figure 6-10. *Removing the scratch with the Healing tool*

5. In the two large shadow areas in the hair, use the same method of mass dust removal as you did in the previous tutorial (when removing dust from the sky area). The only difference here is that you'll set the layer's blend mode to Darken only, because there are light dust specks against a dark background (Figure 6-11).

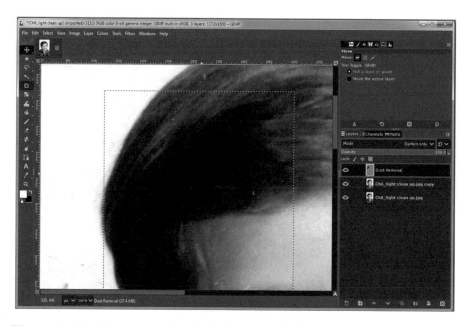

Figure 6-11. *Removing the light dust specks by selecting the Darken only blend mode*

6. The remaining work is just a matter of removing the
    dust specks, using the Healing tool in most cases.
    Larger blemishes are usually better removed with
    the Clone tool (Figure 6-12).

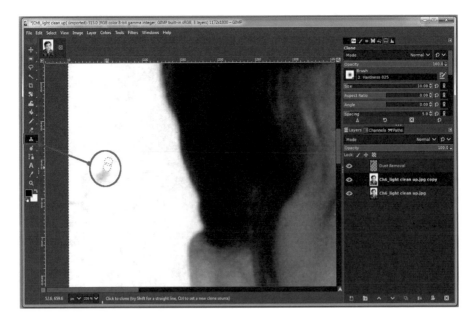

Figure 6-12. *Removing larger imperfections with the Clone tool*

This image had a great deal of dust, some small scratches, and a few other imperfections that required some time and work to remove, but the result is a much cleaner image (Figure 6-13).

Figure 6-13. *The before and after comparison*

Note   Gently cleaning a photograph, slide, or negative with a clean, lint-free cloth can go a long way toward removing loose dust (as we saw in Chapter 2) and can reduce the digital editing workload a great deal.

Tutorial 25: Removing Stains

Stains on old photographs are fairly common, such as in the example in Figure 6-14. Even though it looks like a difficult repair job, this staining can be removed fairly easily by separating the image into its RGB channels.

Figure 6-14. *An old photograph with a rust-colored stain*

To correct this image, follow these steps:

1. Open the image (*Ch6_stained_photo*) found in the Practice Images folder.

2. Open the *Decompose* feature (Colors ➤ Components ➤ Decompose); leave at the default settings and click OK (Figure 6-15).

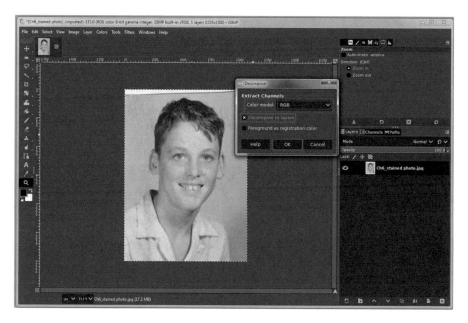

Figure 6-15. *Use the Extract Channels dialog to separate the red, green, and blue color channels as layers*

3. The channels are now extracted as layers in a new image; Figure 6-16 shows a comparison of the red, green, and blue channels (note most of the staining damage is on the blue channel and the least amount is on the red one).

Figure 6-16. *A comparison of the extracted RGB channels*

4.   Change the color mode to RGB (Image ➤ Mode ➤ RGB).

5.   Delete the Green and Blue layers.

6.   Rename the Red layer Background Layer; duplicate it and rename it Clone-Heal Layer.

7.   The rest of the repair work entails cleanup: remove the larger imperfections on the face, shirt, and background, using the Clone and Healing tools on the Clone-Heal Layer (Figure 6-17).

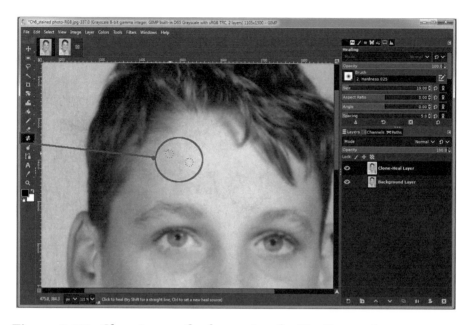

Figure 6-17. *Cleaning up the face using the Healing tool*

8. After the digital cleanup work is completed,
    rebuild the missing area along the top of the image,
    using the Clone tool (C), to give it a straight edge
    (Figure 6-18).

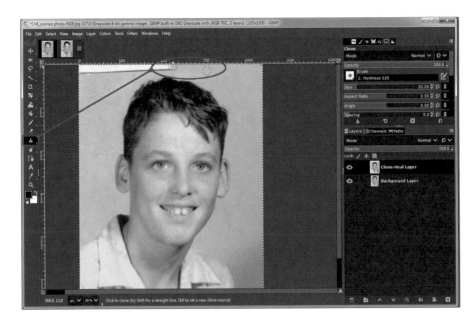

Figure 6-18. *Rebuilding the missing area along the top*

9. Colorize the image by opening the Colorize dialog
   (Colors ➤ Colorize). By using a Hue value of 0.1400
   and the Saturation set to 0.1000, the result is a light
   sepia tone (Figure 6-19).

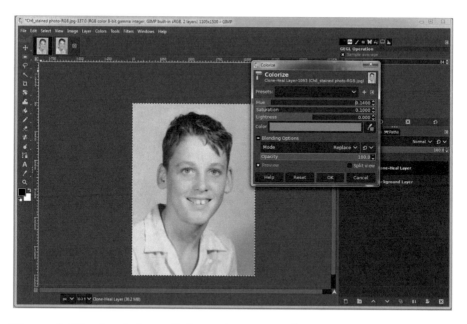

Figure 6-19. *Applying a light sepia tone to the image*

If not for the Red channel being largely undamaged by the stain, this restoration task would have been much more difficult and time-consuming. The result is a nice, cleaned-up image (Figure 6-20). In some color images that are stained, try decomposing the channels into layers to isolate the problem area(s). It is sometimes possible to edit the problematic channel to correct the issue.

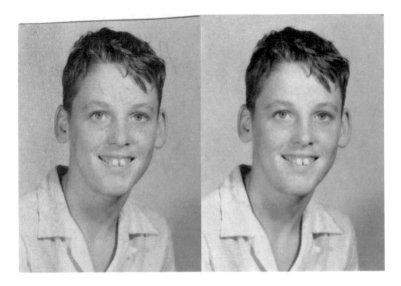

Figure 6-20. *The before and after comparison*

Summary

GIMP is extremely useful for removing dust and other minor imperfections from your photos, negatives, and slides. You can remove dust quickly in areas with unimportant image detail, such as the sky, clouds, solid walls, etc., in a few operations, saving time. The Healing and Clone tools are essential tools for cleaning up stray dust, light imperfections, and scratches. By using the Decompose dialog to extract the color channels into layers, color stains on monochrome or duotone images can often be removed by simply discarding the damaged color layer(s) and utilizing the best one.

GIMP is not limited to minor fixes and light cleanup work. It's a powerful asset for repairing and restoring images with moderate and even severe forms of damage, as you'll see in the next chapter.

CHAPTER 7

Repairing Moderate and Heavy Damage

In This Chapter

- Repairing Moderate Damage
- Repairing Heavy Damage

Repairing Moderate Damage

GIMP is a very capable program for restoring and repairing damaged photographs. Of course, like anything else, photo restoration takes practice and patience to master. The tutorials in this chapter may be a bit challenging if you're a beginner, but stick with it! If your first attempts aren't as good as you'd like them to be, try again. You'll get the hang of it before you know it—if you apply yourself.

© Phillip Whitt 2023
P. Whitt, *Beginning Photo Retouching and Restoration Using GIMP*,
https://doi.org/10.1007/978-1-4842-9265-5_7

Covering Up the Damage

The vast majority of digital restoration is simply "borrowing" from good parts of an image and covering up the damaged portions. Of course, the cover-up must be seamless, to avoid detection. In the tutorials that follow, you'll be patching large areas of damage, as well as using the Clone and Healing tools for the majority of your work. You got a feel for these tools in two of the previous tutorials—now you'll use them to repair damage on a much greater scale.

Tutorial 26: Patching Damaged Areas

The photograph in Figure 7-1 was stuck to the glass of a picture frame (a fairly common issue) which, as you can see, resulted in some nasty torn areas.

Figure 7-1. *Torn areas resulting from sticking to the glass of a picture frame (Image courtesy of the Martin family)*

Sometimes, in these editing situations, using the Clone tool in the larger areas results in a soft, detectable repair, because of the grain and texture in the surrounding image area. In such cases, creating a *patch* will offer a good repair solution.

To correct this image, follow these steps:

1. Open the image (*Ch7_moderate_repair*) found in the Practice Images folder.

2. Duplicate the background layer (Shift + Control + D) and rename it Edit (or Repair) Layer (Figure 7-2).

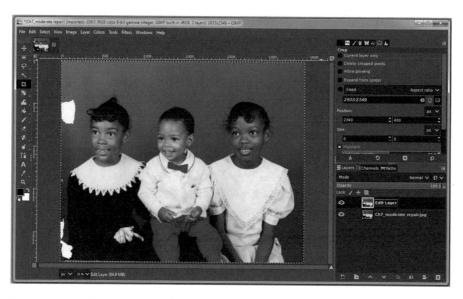

Figure 7-2. *Create a duplicate layer to edit and repair.*

3. Using the Free Select tool (F), set the Feather Edges radius to 30–35 pixels. Make a selection above the large tear (Figure 7-3). Make sure the selection is a good bit larger than the damaged spot.

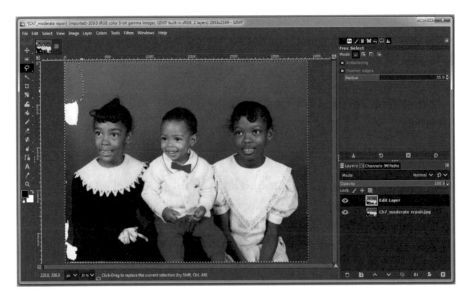

Figure 7-3. *Making a selection above the torn area*

4. We'll now copy this selection and paste it as a new layer (Control + C and Control + V). It will appear as a floating selection in the Layers palette. Right-click the floating selection and select the To New Layer option from the drop-down menu.

5. Rename the layer Patch. Using the Move tool (M), place it over the torn area.

6. Because the background's tone is lighter at the top and gradually darkens toward the bottom, the repair patch will be lighter than the surrounding background. Open the Levels dialog (Colors ➤ Levels) and move the midpoint (gamma) slider to the right until the tone matches. The value should be around 0.90–0.92 (Figure 7-4). You might have

to move the black point slider very slightly to the right. By now, you should have a good match, but experiment as needed.

Figure 7-4. *Using Levels to match the tone of the patch to the surrounding background*

7. Expand the Patch Layer's boundary size to the same size as the image (right-click ➤ *Layer to Image Size*). Using the Eraser tool (Shift + E) with a large, soft brush (about 0.25 hardness), work along the edge of the Patch Layer to blend it in further—be careful not to remove too much.

8. Now we'll create a patch for the smaller damaged areas. Make a selection of the right side of the background, as shown in Figure 7-5, using the Freehand Select tool (F) with the Feather Edges radius set to 30–35 pixels.

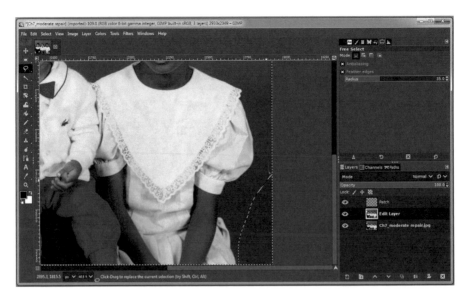

Figure 7-5. *Selecting an area with which to patch the damage on the other side*

9. Copy this selection and paste it as a new layer (Control + C and Control + V)—it will appear as a floating selection in the Layers palette. Right-click the floating selection and select the To New Layer option from the drop-down menu.

10. Rename this layer Patch 2. Use the Flip tool (Shift + F) to reverse the direction of this layer (Figure 7-6).

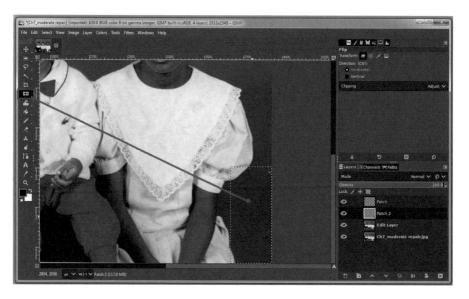

Figure 7-6. *Using the Flip tool to reverse the patch repair layer*

11. Use the Move tool (M) to position the layer over the
     damaged area (Figure 7-7). It will overlap the girl's
     arm, but that's OK for now.

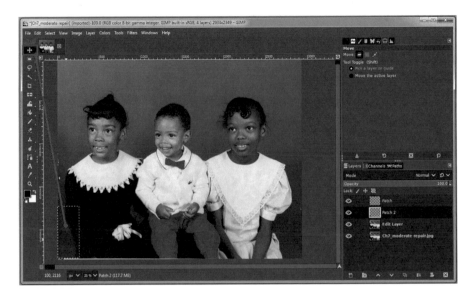

Figure 7-7. *Positioning the repair patch into place*

12. Lower the layer's opacity enough to see the area beneath. Use the Eraser tool (Shift + E) to remove the excess covering the little girl's dress (Figure 7-8). When finished, restore the opacity to 100%.

Figure 7-8. *Removing the excess repair patch*

13.   Open the Levels dialog (*Image Menu* ➤ *Colors* ➤
       Levels) and move the midpoint (gamma) slider to
       the right until the tone matches. The value should
       be around 0.88 (Figure 7-9).

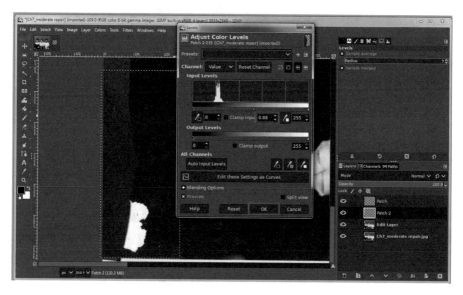

Figure 7-9. *Adjusting the Levels gamma slider to match the tone*

14.   Create a new layer (Shift + Control + N) and name it
       Clone Layer. Move it between the two patch layers
       (Figure 7-10).

Figure 7-10. *Moving the new Clone Layer between the two patch layers*

15. Use the Clone tool (C) with a soft brush on the Clone Layer to fill in the torn area on the girl's dress. The cloning won't extend into the background, because the *Clone Layer* was placed beneath the *Patch 2 Layer* (Figure 7-11). Finish off by cloning away the small section of border on the bottom and any small specks and dust throughout the image.

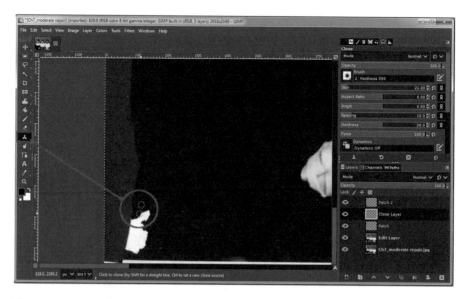

Figure 7-11. *Cloning the torn area*

In just a few steps, we now have an image that is restored and looking like new (Figure 7-12). This patch method also works well in images with missing areas of foliage, bodies of water, etc.

Figure 7-12. *The before and after comparison*

Tutorial 27: Repairing Moderate Damage

Scratches in old photographs (Figure 7-13) are very common in the world of restoration. They can be especially tricky when they occur in facial areas, as in this image. This tutorial will provide you with plenty of practice in using the "dynamic duo" of the tool set—the Clone and Healing tools.

Figure 7-13. *A moderately damaged image with a tear in the background*

To correct this image, follow these steps:

1. Open the image (*Ch7_torn_background*) found in the Practice Images folder.

2. Open the Crop tool (Shift + C) and trim the borders (Figure 7-14).

Figure 7-14. *Trimming the borders*

3. Duplicate the background layer (Shift + Control + D)
    and rename it Edit (or Repair) Layer (Figure 7-15).

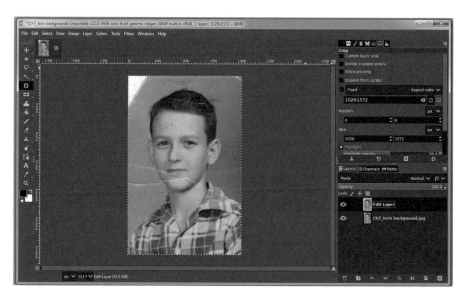

Figure 7-15. *A duplicate layer to edit and repair*

4. Using the Clone tool (C), clean up the area shown
    in Figure 7-16. This area will be used to patch the
    upper-left corner.

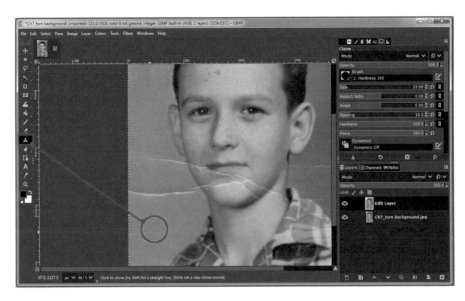

Figure 7-16. *Cleaning an area to borrow for patching the missing corner*

5. Using the Free Select tool (F) with the Feather Edges radius set to about 15 pixels, draw a triangle larger than the missing area on the area you just cleaned up. Copy this selection and paste it as a new layer (Control + C and Control + V)—it will appear as a floating selection in the Layers palette. Right-click the floating selection and select the *To New Layer* option from the drop-down menu (Figure 7-17).

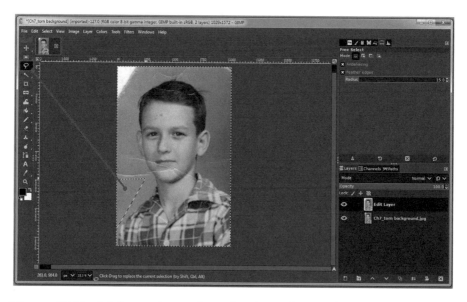

Figure 7-17. *Make a triangular selection of a good area to create a patch for the missing corner*

6. Rename the layer *Corner Patch*.

7. Using the Move tool (M), place it over the torn area. The background's tone will be lighter than the patch. Open the Levels dialog (*Image Menu* ➤ *Colors* ➤ *Levels*) and move the midpoint (gamma) slider slightly to the left until the tone matches. The value should be around 1.10 (Figure 7-18). You might have to move the black point slider very slightly to the right. By now, you should have a good match, but experiment as needed.

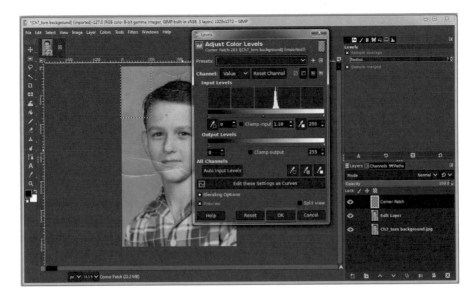

Figure 7-18. *Using Levels to match the tone of the patch to the surrounding background*

8. Duplicate the background layer (Shift + Control + D) and rename it *Edit (or Repair) Layer*.

9. Using the Healing tool (H), start working on the small scratches in the hair. The Healing tool will blend in the surrounding texture for a seamless repair (Figure 7-19).

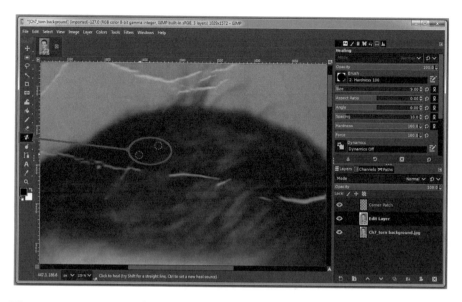

Figure 7-19. *Using the Healing tool to remove the scratches in the hair*

Larger areas are often better repaired with the Clone tool (C), so alternate between the two as needed (Figure 7-20).

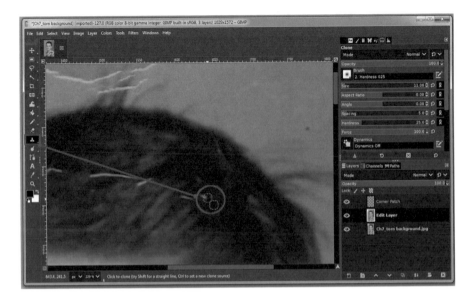

Figure 7-20. *Using the Clone tool for repairing a wider scratch*

10. When finished with the hair, move on to the face.
     Use the Clone tool (C) to remove the stains, as
     shown in Figure 7-21.

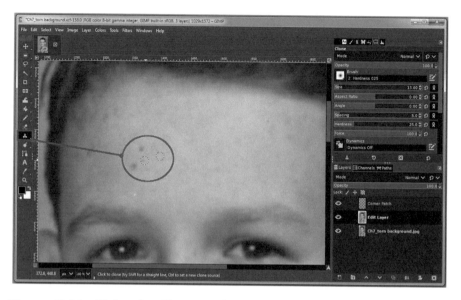

Figure 7-21. *Using the Clone tool to remove stains*

11. Now, it will get a bit tricky—the damage around the
     mouth has to be addressed and may require more
     than one attempt. Create a new layer (above the
     Repair Layer) and name it *Lip Repair Layer*. Use
     the Clone tool (C), and with a soft brush rebuild the
     missing area below the lower lip (Figure 7-22).

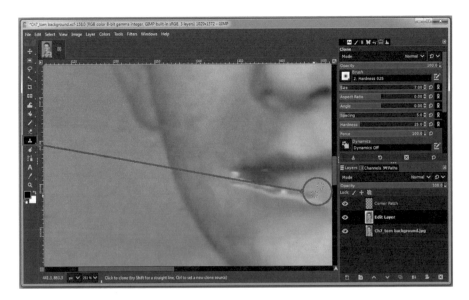

Figure 7-22. *Using the Clone tool to repair the damaged area around the lip*

12. Use the Blur/Sharpen tool (Shift + U), set to Blur, to smooth out the cloned areas and blend the repair in.

13. Use the Dodge/Burn tool (Shift + D), set to Burn, and an exposure of about 15–20 to gently replace the shadow that may have been removed during the repair work (Figure 7-23).

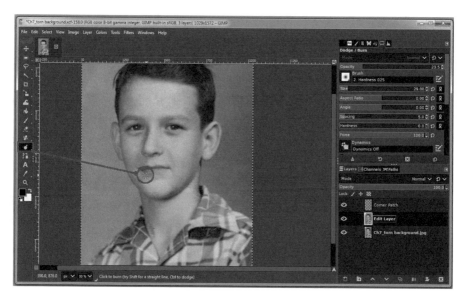

Figure 7-23. *Replacing the shadow with the Burn tool*

14.   After you repair the mouth area, clean up the rest of
the photograph with the Healing and Clone tools.
The next thing we have to do is smooth out the
background some. Using the Free Select tool (F)
with the Feather Edges radius set to about 35 pixels,
draw around the subject, as shown in Figure 7-24.

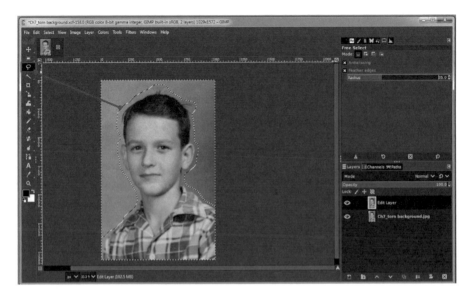

Figure 7-24. *Draw a freehand selection*

15. Merge the layer named Corner Patch on to the Edit layer (right-click + Merge Down).

16. Right-click the Edit Layer, and select *Layer to Image Size*.

17. Copy the selection and paste it as a new layer (Edit ➤ Copy, then Edit ➤ Paste as ➤ New Layer).

18. Deactivate the selection (Select ➤ None).

19. Open the Gaussian Blur dialog (*Filters ➤ Blur ➤ Gaussian Blur*). Set the Blur radius to about 15 (both Size X and Size Y); leave the other settings as their default positions (Figure 7-25).

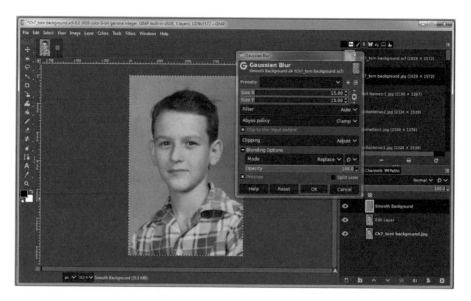

Figure 7-25. *Smoothing the background using the Gaussian Blur filter*

20. The background is now much smoother, but the texture is gone and must be replaced. Open the RGB Noise dialog (*Filters ➤ Noise ➤ RGB Noise*). Deselect the Independent RGB option and set the value to 0.015 and the Opacity to 75%, then click OK (Figure 7-26).

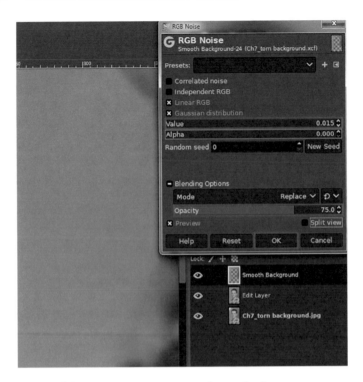

Figure 7-26. *Adding some noise to replace the lost texture*

21. Hide the background layer and merge the visible layers (right-click in the Layers palette and choose Merge Visible Layers from the drop-down menu). Turn the background layer's visibility back on.

22. The finishing touch is now to boost the contrast just a little. Open the Curves dialog (*Image Menu ➤ Colors ➤ Colors ➤ Curves*). Make a slight "S" curve, as shown in Figure 7-27.

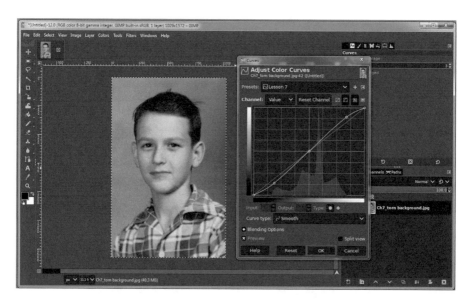

Figure 7-27. *Boosting the contrast with a slight "S" curve*

There's quite an improvement in the end result (Figure 7-28).

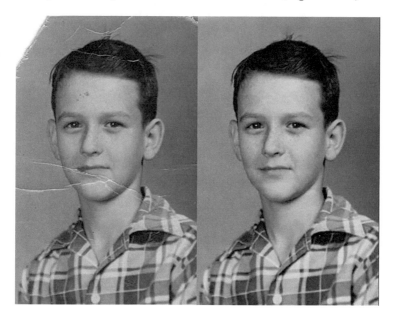

Figure 7-28. *The before and after comparison*

Repairing Heavy Damage

Over the years, it seems that most of the restoration work that comes my way results from damage like that on the image shown in Figure 7-29 (or worse). Heavy damage such as this requires extensive use of the Healing and Clone tools. In addition, we'll also rebuild part of the image rather than try to repair it.

Figure 7-29. *An image with heavy damage*

Tutorial 28: Repairing Heavy Damage

To correct this image, follow these steps:

1. Open the image (*Ch7_heavy_damage*) found in the Practice Images folder.

2. Duplicate the background layer (Shift + Control + D) and rename it Edit (or Repair) Layer.

3. Create a new layer (Shift + Control + N) and name it Sky—we'll start the repair process by replacing the sky in this image (Figure 7-30).

Figure 7-30. *A layer that will be used for replacing the sky*

4. With the Antialias box ticked, and Feather Edges set to 2, use the Free Select tool (F) to select the sky— just start at the left and follow along the edge of the rooflines (Figure 7-31).

Figure 7-31. *Use the Free Select tool to make a selection around the sky*

5. After the sky has been selected, open the Color
    Picker tool (O) and sample the areas shown
    (Figure 7-32); after sampling, press X to ensure the
    Foreground color is the darker gray and that the
    Background color is the slightly lighter gray.

Figure 7-32. *Set the Foreground and Background colors to the grays shown*

6. We'll now create a replacement sky—using the Gradient tool (G), drag from the top of the image about two-thirds of the way down as shown in Figure 7-33; press Enter to commit the action.

Figure 7-33. *Use the Gradient tool to draw a replacement sky*

7. We'll now add a small bit of noise to the sky; open
    the RGB Noise dialog (Filters ➤ Noise ➤ RGB
    Noise); disable the Independent RGB setting and set
    the value to 0.015, then click OK (Figure 7-34).

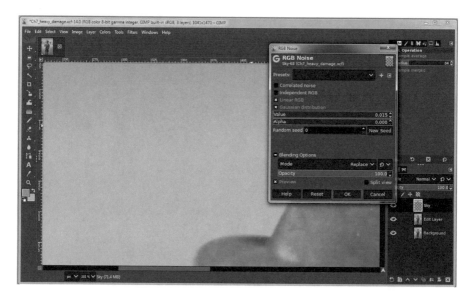

Figure 7-34. *Use the RGB Noise dialog to add a small amount of noise to the gradient*

8. Create a new layer (Shift + Control + N) and name it Clone Layer; move it above the Edit Layer.

9. Using the Clone tool (C), start repairing the damage as shown in Figure 7-35.

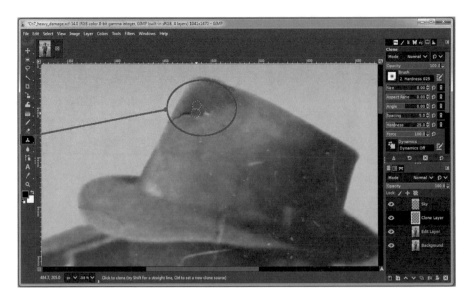

Figure 7-35. *Use the Clone tool to begin repairing the damage*

Note   There are a lot of small dust specks in this image. Using the Blur/Sharpen tool (set to the Blur Convolve Type) with a small brush diameter can remove these fairly quickly and easily.

---

10.   After the man's hat is repaired, you can then move on to the face (Figure 7-36).

Figure 7-36. *Once the man's hat is repaired, you can then work on the face*

11. Repairing the large area of damage in the beach houses will be a challenge; it will require using the Clone tool to rebuild the areas to cover the damage (Figure 7-37); repair the rest of the image using the Clone tool (you may also find the Healing tool helpful in some parts of the image)—leave the lower-left corner as is for now.

Figure 7-37. *Use the Clone tool to reconstruct damaged areas in the beach houses*

12. Toggle the visibility of the background layer off (by clicking the eye-shaped icon); merge the visible layers (right-click + Merge Visible Layers).

13. Restore the background layer's visibility.

14. With the Feather Edges set to 5.0, use the Free Select tool (F) to draw a selection as shown in Figure 7-38.

Figure 7-38. *Use the Free Select tool*

15. Copy the selected area to a new layer (Edit ➤ Copy, then Edit ➤ Paste as New Layer).

16. Use the Move tool (M) to move the copied layer into place to cover the missing corner (Figure 7-39); use the Clone tool to eliminate any repeating pattern that may result.

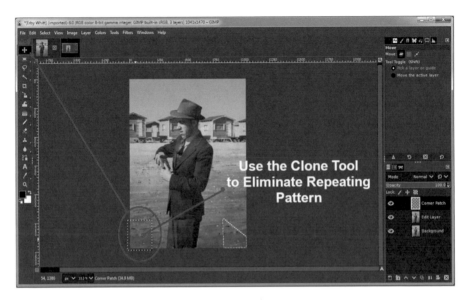

Figure 7-39. *Use the Move tool to move the pasted layer over the missing corner and the Clone tool to eliminate any repeating pattern*

17. Merge the pasted layer down on to the Edit Image.

18. The last thing is to sharpen the image just a bit; open the Unsharp Mask dialog (Filters ➤ Enhance ➤ Sharpen (Unsharp Mask)) and set the Radius to 2.5, then click OK (Figure 7-40).

Figure 7-40. *Sharpen the image a bit using the Unsharp Mask dialog*

This is a tough project. If your results are less than optimal, just try again. Remember, restoration takes practice. If your results closely resemble the example in Figure 7-41, congratulations!

Figure 7-41. *The before and after comparison*

Summary

GIMP is extremely useful for fixing damaged images. The tools at your disposal will let you repair cracks, tears, and all types of damage. With time and practice, you'll be able to salvage images you thought beyond hope. If you plan to offer image restoration as part of your professional services, your customers will appreciate you all the more!

PART IV

Retouching Faces, Fun Projects, Preserving Your Images

CHAPTER 8

Editing Portraits and Recomposing Images

In This Chapter

- Retouching Portraits
- Recomposing Images

Retouching Portraits

Even the best of portraits can often benefit from a little digital magic. GIMP is ideal for touch-up work and enhancing the best attributes of the photographed subject while diminishing the distractions that can overpower a great image. Imperfections such as wrinkles and crow's feet can be lessened. Skin can be made smoother and more radiant. Dull or yellowing teeth can be digitally brightened and enhanced.

© Phillip Whitt 2023
P. Whitt, *Beginning Photo Retouching and Restoration Using GIMP*,
https://doi.org/10.1007/978-1-4842-9265-5_8

Diminishing Imperfections and Removing Distractions

My approach to retouching is to do it as sparingly as possible. When it's overdone, it can look a bit artificial. Retouching can take a few years away from a portrait's subject, but trying to make someone in their mid-40s look 23 might not be the best approach. The objective is to minimize distractions and imperfections and to emphasize the best attributes (and maintain the character) of the person in the photograph. It pays to take some time to study the image and determine your course of action for the necessary editing.

Figure 8-1 illustrates the distractions and imperfections that are present and a strategy for dealing with them, to bring out the best in this image.

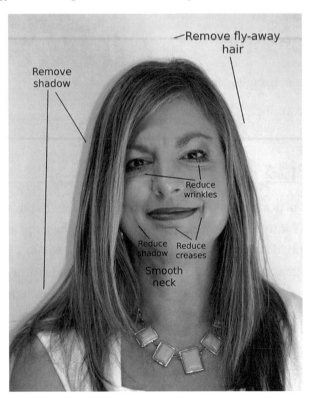

Figure 8-1. *Take some time to determine your course of action*

Tutorial 29: Portrait Retouch

In the image you are about to retouch, the key is to reduce the severity of the facial issues (seen in Figure 8-1) but not to completely eliminate them, to prevent looking like plastic surgery was performed.

The Wavelets Decompose plug-in must be installed to follow this tutorial.

To edit this image, follow these steps:

1. Open the image (*Ch8_retouch_portrait*) located in the Practice Images folder. Duplicate the background layer and rename it Retouch Layer.

2. Create a new layer (Shift + Control + N) and name it Shadow/Flyaway Hair Removal (Figure 8-2).

Figure 8-2. *Creating layers on which to perform retouching tasks*

3. Use the Clone tool (C) with the Sample Merged option enabled to remove the stray flyaway hairs on the Shadow/Flyaway Hair Removal layer (Figure 8-3). Set the brush size just slightly larger than the hair strand on lone hairs. Increase the brush size to remove clusters of hair.

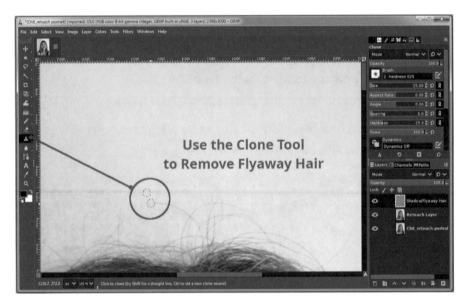

Figure 8-3. *Use the Clone tool to remove flyaway hair*

4. Use the Clone tool (C) to remove the light shadow (and flyaway hairs) on the side of the woman's head. Resample often as you work down (Figure 8-4). Use the brush preset Hardness 050, with a brush hardness of about 25.

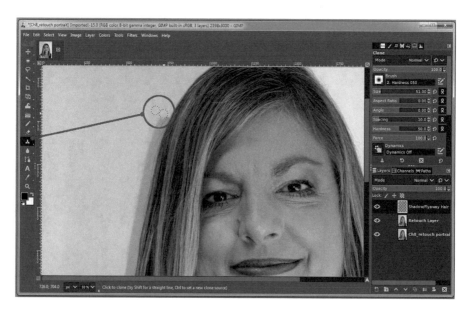

Figure 8-4. *Removing the shadow and flyaway hairs using the Clone tool*

5. This procedure may give the repaired area a slightly smooth appearance, as compared to the surrounding background, most noticeable when viewing zoomed in. If necessary, add a minimum amount of noise (Image Menu ➤ Filters ➤ Noise ➤ RGB Noise). Uncheck the Correlated noise and Independent RGB options and set the noise to the lowest setting of 0.01, then click OK (Figure 8-5).

Figure 8-5. *Add a minimum amount of noise to the Clone/Flyaway Hair Removal layer, if needed*

6. When the cloning is completed, merge the Clone/
    Shadow/Flyaway Hair Removal layer down.
    Figure 8-6 reveals an improved image, as a result of
    the removal of the shadow and flyaway hair.

Figure 8-6. *Removing the distracting flyaway hair and the shadow improves this image*

7. Now it's time to do some retouching on the face. Open the Wavelets Decompose dialog (Image Menu ➤ Filters ➤ Enhance ➤ Wavelets Decompose). Use the default option of creating five scales. The Wavelet scales contain varying degrees of edge detail (Figure 8-7).

Figure 8-7. *Wavelet scales*

8.   Use the Free Select tool (F) with the Feather Edges radius set to 10 pixels to draw around the under-eye creases and the two near the mouth (Figure 8-8).

Figure 8-8. *Selections made around the harsher areas to be retouched*

9. Click Wavelet scale 3, and apply the Gaussian Blur filter (Image Menu ➤ Filters ➤ Blur ➤ Gaussian Blur) with the blur radius (verticalX and horizontalY) set to 40.

10. Click Wavelet scale 4, and reapply the Gaussian Blur (Control + F). The under-eye creases are noticeably diminished. The mouth creases look a bit less harsh (Figure 8-9).

Figure 8-9. *The retouched areas looking a bit better*

11. Use the Free Select tool (F) to draw around the
forehead, cheeks, chin, and neck. Click Wavelet
scale 3 and apply the Gaussian Blur filter, using a
blur radius of 15 pixels (Figure 8-10).

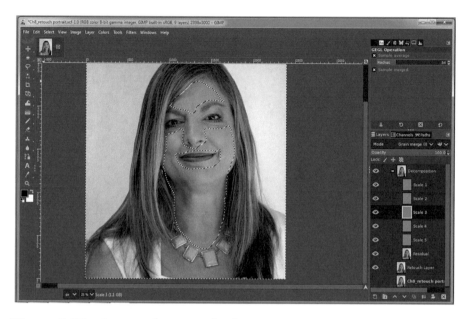

Figure 8-10. *Areas to be smoothed*

12. Hide the background layer and merge the remaining visible layers (Merge Visible Layers)—make sure the Merge within active group only option is unchecked.

13. Add a new layer (Shift + Control + N) and change the blend mode to Soft Light.

14. Fill the layer with 50% gray, and using the Airbrush tool (A) with the opacity set to 15 and white as the active color, paint along the deeper creases in the face and neck to reduce the severity of the shadow (Figure 8-11).

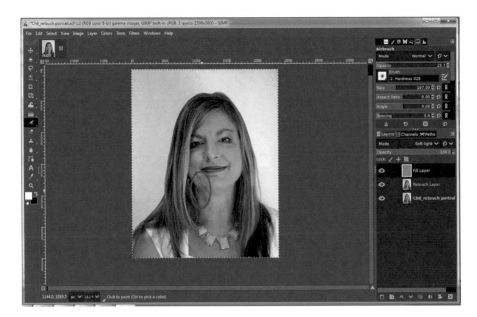

Figure 8-11. *Using a Soft Light layer and the Airbrush tool to lighten the shadows*

15. Use the Healing tool (H) with the opacity set to
     35 to reduce the bump around the nose and the
     blemishes on the neck (Figure 8-12).

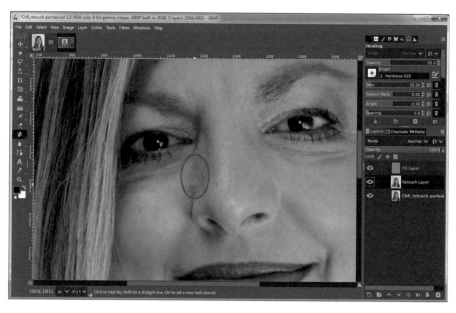

Figure 8-12. *Final touches using the Healing tool*

16. In the final result, the distractions are removed, and the imperfections are diminished (Figure 8-13).

Figure 8-13. *The before and after comparison*

Tutorial 30: Brightening Teeth

Over time, our teeth can become dingy and stained from consumption of coffee, wine, tobacco, and various other substances. Age is also a factor—most people at the age of 60 don't have the bright, white smile of an 18-year-old. Many images can benefit from some digital "cosmetic dentistry." We'll see how GIMP will subtly brighten and whiten the teeth in Figure 8-14.

As in facial retouching, use a light touch in brightening teeth, or you'll end up with results that will be obvious and appear fake or won't look right to the people who know the person in the photograph.

Figure 8-14. *A great smile that can be further enhanced with GIMP*

To edit this image, follow these steps:

1. Open the image (*Ch8_brighten_teeth*) located in the Practice Images folder.

2. Use the Free Select tool (F) with the Feather Edges radius set to 1.0 and make a selection around the teeth (Figure 8-15).

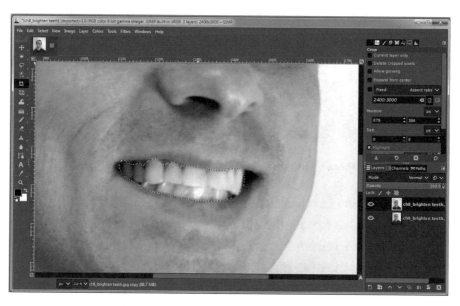

Figure 8-15. *Make a selection around the teeth*

3. Copy and paste the selection (Control + C + V) and convert the floating selection to a new layer (Shift + Control + N). Rename it Teeth.

4. Open the Hue-Saturation dialog (Image Menu ➤ Colors ➤ Hue Saturation). Select yellow as the primary color and adjust the slider to about 40, then click OK. This will reduce some of the yellow just a bit (Figure 8-16).

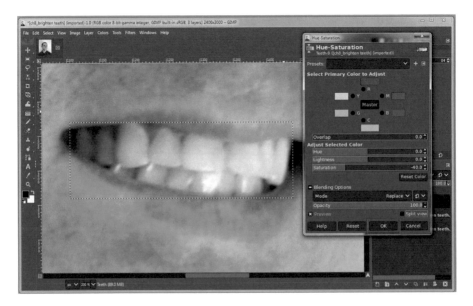

Figure 8-16. *Reduce the yellow, using the Hue-Saturation dialog*

5. Open the Levels dialog (Image Menu ➤ Colors ➤
    Levels) and move the midpoint slider to the left
    until the value is about 1.40, then click OK. This will
    lighten the teeth just slightly (Figure 8-17).

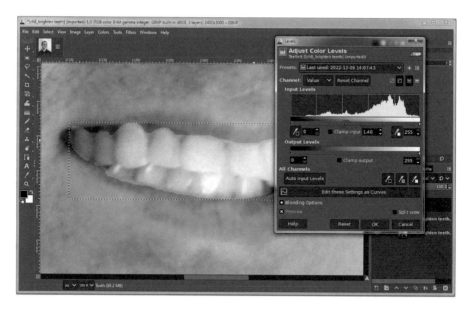

Figure 8-17. *Use the Levels dialog to brighten the teeth slightly*

6. With a brush about 12 pixels in diameter and a hardness of about 50%, use the Eraser tool (Shift + E) to clean up any stray pixels around the teeth (Figure 8-18).

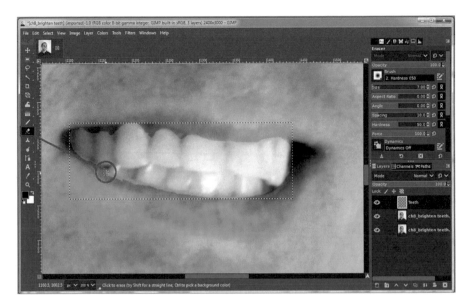

Figure 8-18. *Use the Eraser tool to clean up any stray pixels around the teeth*

We can see in Figure 8-19 that the teeth are noticeably improved, but without the end result being overpowering. Subtlety is key when working with the color and brightness in teeth.

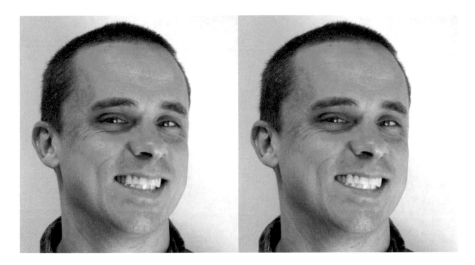

Figure 8-19. *The before and after comparison*

Recomposing Images

Recomposing portraits or important photographs is common part of image editing. People become very emotionally attached to certain photographs, but they may contain an ugly background or an in-law, ex-spouse, or some other unwelcome person or element that the owner of the photograph finds unpleasant.

The two most frequently requested services I receive are replacing backgrounds and removing people from portraits. On occasion, I'll receive a request to add someone to an image.

Recomposing an image consists mainly of covering up unwanted image data with replacement data and working with it to create a realistic outcome. The tutorials that follow demonstrate two background replacement methods and one involving removing someone from a snapshot.

Replacing Backgrounds

In my line of work as a retouch artist, replacing backgrounds is one of the most frequently requested editing services I provide. Sometimes, it's because there's only one existing photograph of a certain person, and the client would like a "studio" version of the image, such as a muslin background behind the subject. Other times, the client desires a reimagined version of a photographic scene. Sometimes, it's just a busy, cluttered, and distracting background spoiling the photo.

Tutorial 31: Replacing a Background (No. 1)

The image shown in Figure 8-20 is scanned from a photograph that I shot in 1993 (in the days few people could afford Photoshop). It has a great subject, but the elements in the background (the open garage, orange road construction barrel, street, etc.) detract from what is otherwise a good portrait.

Figure 8-20. *A cluttered background detracts from an otherwise*
good image

In the following tutorial, you'll extract the young woman's image and
place it on a more suitable background, resulting in a much better portrait.

To edit this image, follow these steps:

1. Open the image (*Ch8_background_change_1*)
    located in the Practice Images folder. (The image
    you'll use as the new background accompanies the
    practice image.)

2. Use the Free Select tool (F) to draw a loose outline
    around the young woman. It's OK to err outside of
    the edge; that will be refined shortly (Figure 8-21).

Figure 8-21. *Draw a selection around the subject*

3. Switch to the Quick Mask mode (Shift + Q). With black as the active color and the brush preset hardness of 050, paint along the edge to complete the selection (Figure 8-22). Be sure to paint the areas of the background that show through the hair and between the arm and dress.

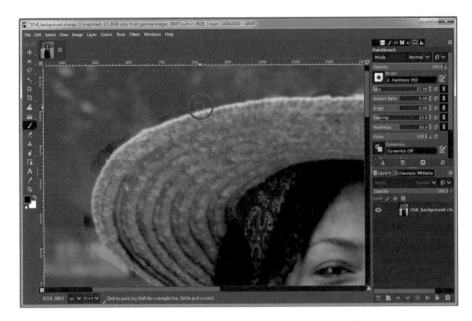

Figure 8-22. *Paint along the edge to complete the selection*

4. Deactivate the Quick Mask mode (Shift + Q) to
    switch back to the "marching ant" selection. We'll
    now copy the selected subject to its own layer
    (Control + C and Control + V). Change the floating
    selection to a layer (Shift + Control + N). Rename the
    layer Isolated Girl.

5. Hide the background layer by clicking the eyeball
    icon (Figure 8-23). If there are any residual pixels left
    to remove, add a layer mask to the Isolated Girl layer
    (right-click + Add Layer Mask). Leave the layer mask
    at the default settings.

Figure 8-23. *The isolated subject*

6. Using black as the active color, click the layer mask
    to make it active, and paint on the stray pixels to
    make them transparent.

7. Open the image we'll use for the new background
    (*Ch8_sunlight_through trees*). Copy it to the
    clipboard (Control + C).Paste it as a new layer into
    the project (Image Menu ➤ Edit ➤ Paste As ➤ New
    Layer). Rename it *New Background* and move it
    under the *Isolated Girl* layer (Figure 8-24).

Figure 8-24. *The new background layer put into place*

8. For a slightly more realistic depth-of-field look
    effect, the background should not be as sharp as
    the subject. Blur the background just a bit with the
    Gaussian Blur dialog (Filters ➤ Blur ➤ Gaussian
    Blur), using a radius of 0.75 pixels (Image Menu
    ➤ Filters ➤ Blur ➤ Gaussian Blur), as shown in
    Figure 8-25.

9. After blurring, the background looks very smooth
    when compared to the subject. Using the G'MIC
    plug-in, add some film grain to the New Background
    layer to create a better match. After experimenting,
    I preferred the result I got using the default settings
    and checking the Colored grain option (Figure 8-25).

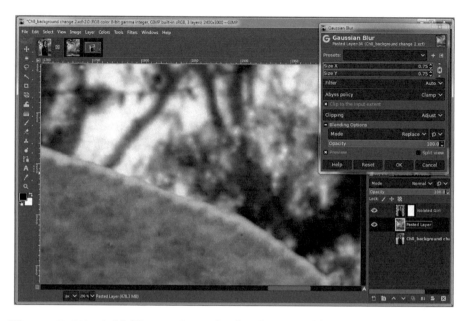

Figure 8-25. *Add film grain to the background layer to match the grain in the subject*

The end result is a much more aesthetically pleasing portrait. A different background can make a huge difference (Figure 8-26).

Figure 8-26. *The before and after comparison*

Tutorial 32: Replacing a Background (No. 2)

The image shown in Figure 8-27 is actually a decent portrait. Most people would probably like it as is, but sometimes customers will request something a little more stylish, such as a muslin studio-style scenic or studio background. In this lesson, we'll place the subject on a digital background I created several years ago. This young woman has some tight curls in her hair, so this tutorial will involve a little more refinement than the previous one.

Figure 8-27. *A portrait that will receive a studio-style replacement background*

To edit this image, follow these steps:

1. Open the image (*Ch8_background_change_2*) located in the Practice Images folder. (The image you'll use as the new background accompanies the practice image.)

2. Duplicate the background layer *twice.* Rename the uppermost layer Edit Layer (Figure 8-28).

Figure 8-28. *For this tutorial, the background layer will be duplicated twice*

3. Add a transparency (in the form of an alpha channel) to the Edit Layer (Image Menu ➤ Layer ➤ Transparency ➤ Add Alpha Channel).

4. Open the Threshold dialog (Image Menu ➤ Colors ➤ Threshold). Leave the slider at the default setting (Figure 8-29), then click OK.

Figure 8-29. *The Threshold dialog*

5. Reverse the black and white colors (Image Menu
   ➤ Colors ➤ Invert). Using white as the active color
   and a hard brush, fill in the black gaps within the
   inverted silhouette (Figure 8-30).

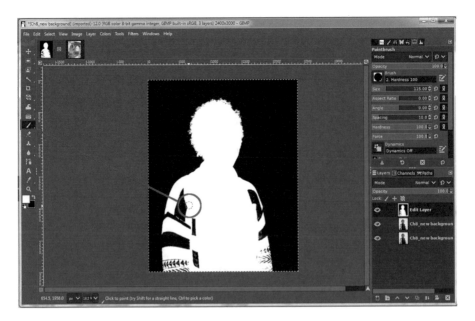

Figure 8-30. *Paint in the inverted silhouette with white*

6. Lower the opacity of the *Edit Layer* to reveal the
    image underneath sufficiently to use it as a guide
    to paint the edges of the bands in the sweater and
    to refine any jagged edges around the subject
    (Figure 8-31); when finished, raise the opacity back
    to 100%.

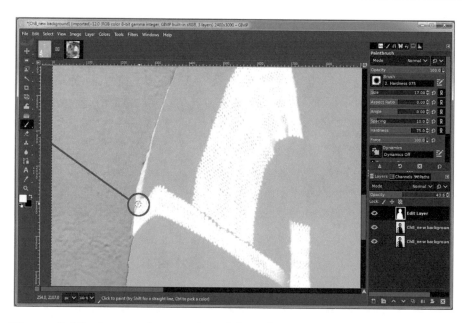

Figure 8-31. *Lower the opacity of the Edit Layer to reveal the edge in the bands of the sweater along which to paint*

7. Cut the Edit Layer to the clipboard (Control + X). Using the Select By Color tool (Shift + O), click in the white area of the Edit Layer; make sure the Antialias box is checked and use a Threshold setting of 8.0 (Figure 8-32).

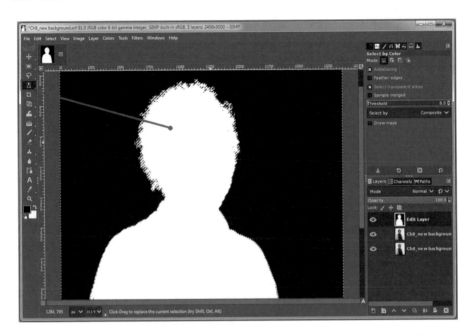

Figure 8-32. *Select the white area using the Select By Color tool*

8. Add a layer mask to the background layer copy
    (Image Menu ➤ Layer ➤ Mask ➤ Add Layer
    Mask). Make the duplicate background layer active
    by clicking the preview thumbnail as shown in
    Figure 8-33.

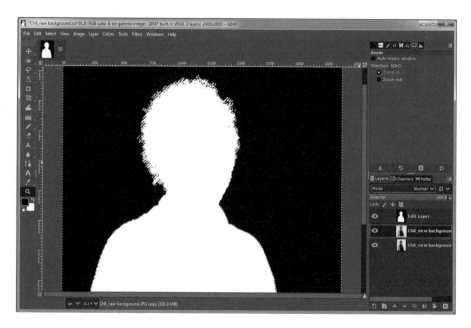

Figure 8-33. *Make the duplicate background layer active by clicking the preview thumbnail*

9. Copy the subject (Edit ➤ Copy). Click the layer mask to make it active, and paste the extracted subject (Control + V). The pixels of the original background have been made transparent.

10. Open the new background image titled Ch8_studio_ background using the Open as Layers option (File ➤ Open as Layers ➤ Ch8_studio_background) found in the Practice Images folder; it should be above the duplicate background layer as shown in Figure 8-34.

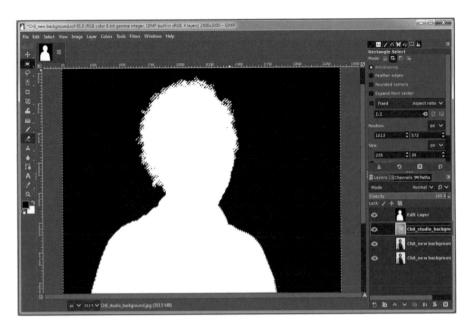

Figure 8-34. *Open the image (Ch8_studio_background) to use as a new background layer*

11. Copy it to the clipboard (Control + C). Paste it as a new layer into the project (Image Menu ➤ Edit ➤ Paste As ➤ New Layer). Rename it Studio Background and move it under the background layer copy. Paste the copied pixels into a new layer (Edit ➤ Paste As ➤ New Layer).

12. Use the Dodge/Burn tool (Shift + D) with the burn option selected and the exposure set to 75 and darken the curls with the light fringes. Turn the visibility of the background and Edit layers off (Figure 8-35).

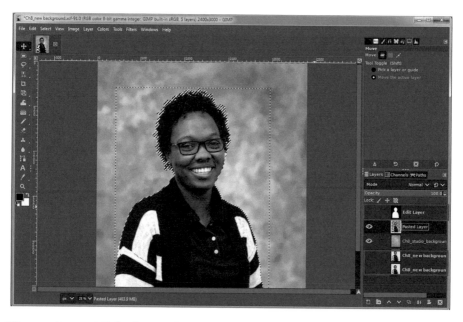

Figure 8-35. *Hide the visibility of the Edit Layer and the background layers*

13. Click the layer mask to make it active and use the Blur/Sharpen tool with the blur option selected to soften the edges slightly. Set the opacity to 100 and the rate to 20. Deactivate the selection (Select ➤ None).

14. Add a minimum amount of noise to the Studio Background (Image Menu ➤ Filters ➤ Noise ➤ RGB Noise). Use the lowest setting, with the Independent RGB option unchecked. Check around the image and use the Eraser tool to clean up any excess pixels (Figure 8-36); use the Blur tool to smooth any jagged parts of the edge.

Figure 8-36. *Use the Eraser tool to remove excess pixels*

This method of replacing the background preserves all but the finest hairs. (I used a difficult subject here; most hair will be a little easier to handle.) The result is a portrait that looks like it was taken in a studio (Figure 8-37).

Figure 8-37. *The before and after comparison*

Removing People

As mentioned previously, clients will often request having someone digitally removed from a treasured photograph. This task is basically just a matter of borrowing image data from one part of the picture to cover up the person to be taken out of the image.

Tutorial 33: Removing a Person

The example in Figure 8-38 is a Polaroid photograph of my late brother, Glenn, taken in the late 1980s or early 1990s. I've always loved this picture, because it shows a rarely seen playful aspect of Glenn's personality. I don't have many photos of him by himself, so I decided to edit this one, so that I can now have one of my favorite ones (and it makes a great tutorial).

Figure 8-38. *A photograph of my late brother, Glenn, soon to be alone in this image*

To edit this image, follow these steps:

1. Open the image (*Ch8_remove_girl*) located in the Practice Images folder.

2. Duplicate the background layer and rename it Edit Layer (Figure 8-39).

Figure 8-39. *Create a duplicate layer to edit*

3. Using the Free Select tool (F) and the Feather Edges radius set to 10 pixels, draw a selection around the area on the right side of the image (Figure 8-40).

Figure 8-40. *Make a selection around the dark area to create a patch to cover the woman*

4. Copy and paste (Control + C and Control + V) as a floating selection. Change the floating selection into a new layer (Shift + Control + N). Expand the layer's boundary size to match the image size (Image Menu ➤ Layer ➤ Layer to Image Size). Rename the layer Patch 1).

5. Use the Move tool (M) to move the patch over the woman's face. Some of it will cover part of the man's hair and sombrero, but that's OK for now (Figure 8-41).

Figure 8-41. *Move the patch into place*

6. The patch layer will be a little darker than the surrounding image area. Open the Levels dialog (Image Menu ➤ Colors ➤ Levels). Move the white point slider to the left to lighten the patch layer slightly and create a better tonal match. The value should be around 230 (Figure 8-42).

Figure 8-42. *Use the Levels dialog to create a better tonal match between the patch and surrounding area*

7. Lower the opacity of the patch layer to about 50%, to see underneath. Use the Erase tool (Shift + E) with the brush set to 050 to remove the pixels covering the man's hair and sombrero (Figure 8-43).

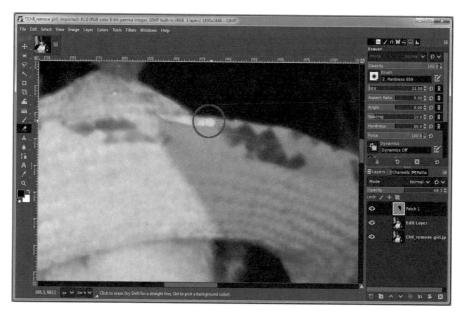

Figure 8-43. *Use the Erase tool to remove the excess pixels from the patch layer*

8. Create a new layer (Shift + Control + N) and name it Clone. Using the Clone tool (C), with the Sample Merged option box checked, clone over the remaining image of the woman (Figure 8-44).

Figure 8-44. *Use the Clone tool to remove what remains of the woman*

9. Use the Free Select tool on the Edit Layer to draw an area on the sleeve just under the hand. Copy and paste (Control + C and Control + V) as a floating selection. Change the floating selection into a new layer (Shift + Control + N). Expand the layer's boundary size to match the image size (Image Menu ➤ Layer ➤ Layer to Image Size). Rename the layer Pattern (or Sleeve, if you prefer) (Figure 8-45).

Figure 8-45. *Make a selection around the sleeve to make a patch to cover the woman's hand*

10. Move the layer into place over the hand. Use the Erase tool (Shift + E) to remove the excess. Use the Clone tool (C) for touch-up work and to remove the rest of the hand on the Clone layer (Figure 8-46).

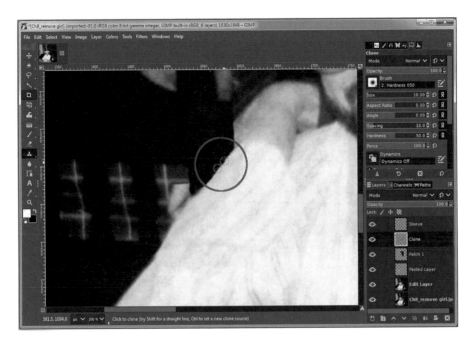

Figure 8-46.   *Clone out the rest of the hand*

11.   Use the Clone tool (C) to remove the plant and the person's head (which is slightly visible) in the background (Figure 8-47).

Figure 8-47. *Clone out the plant and the portion of the person's head in the background*

12. Crop the image a little tighter to remove some of the excess area (Figure 8-48).

Figure 8-48. *Crop the excess area from the image*

Note   Normally, I crop images earlier in the editing process, but in a case such as this, it's necessary to borrow from other parts of the image to cover the object or person to be removed. Leave as much image information available as possible for this purpose, then crop the image after the editing has been done.

Careful patching and cloning results in a very nice edited snapshot and a plausible image (Figure 8-49).

Figure 8-49. *The before and after comparison*

Summary

GIMP is a very useful program for correcting flaws and retouching portraits, so that people can look their best. It's great for isolating people (or pets, for that matter) and digitally replacing backgrounds and changing scenery. With GIMP, you'll be able to remove unwanted people or objects from images and end up with great results.

CHAPTER 9

Sharpening Images

In This Chapter

- Sharpening—The Final Step
- The Unsharp Mask Filter
- High Pass Sharpening

Sharpening—The Final Step

In many instances, the images you work with will benefit from a little sharpening. After you complete your retouching/restoration steps, sharpening should be the final step in the editing process. Images are also generally sharpened after downscaling (such as those being prepared for use on the Web). This process will not correct images that are out of focus and blurry, but it will improve images that are slightly soft, such as scanned photographs. Some scanners employ an auto-sharping feature, which may provide satisfactory results. However, to exercise more control over the sharpening process, the auto feature should be disabled. Figure 9-1 shows an example of how a scanned photograph can be improved with just a slight amount of sharpening. Notice how the catchlights in the eyes are just a bit crisper and brighter.

© Phillip Whitt 2023
P. Whitt, *Beginning Photo Retouching and Restoration Using GIMP*,
https://doi.org/10.1007/978-1-4842-9265-5_9

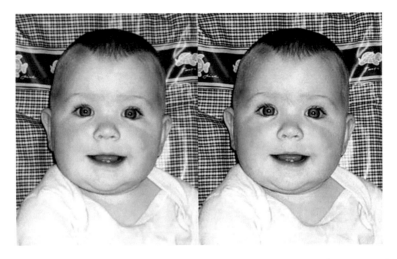

Figure 9-1. *A before and after example of a scanned photograph slightly sharpened*

The Unsharp Mask Filter

This filter's name sounds counterintuitive to making an image look sharper, but it's derived from a photographic process that uses a blurred, or "unsharp," mask of the original positive image. This mask is combined with the negative image, creating a result that has greater apparent sharpness.

The Unsharp Mask filter increases contrast between neighboring dark and light pixels, which in actuality creates the illusion of increased sharpness.

The *Unsharp Mask* dialog is nested within the filters (Image Menu ➤ Filters ➤ Enhance ➤ Unsharp Mask). There are three setting options in the dialog: Radius, Amount, and Threshold. Figure 9-2 shows a split view of a rose with the Unsharp Mask filter using the default settings in place.

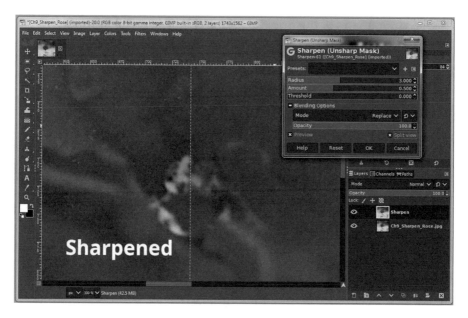

Figure 9-2. *The setting options in the Unsharp Mask dialog*

1. *Radius*: The slider and input boxes (0.1–120)
   determine how many pixels on either side of an
   edge are affected by sharpening.

2. *Amount*: The slider and input boxes (0.00–5.00)
   determine the intensity of the sharpening effect.

3. *Threshold*: This allows you to protect areas that are
   similar in tone from sharpening. Areas of smooth
   tonal transition can be protected from sharpening,
   minimizing the creation of unwanted blemishes or
   artifacts.

The main disadvantage of using the Unsharp Mask filter is that the
effect can accentuate film grain and digital noise and create unsightly
artifacts around the edges in the image. This filter can be somewhat
destructive, so I recommend applying it with a light touch. Figure 9-3

shows a comparison of the original scanned image, using the default settings of the Unsharp Mask filter (which, in this case, is about the right amount), and an example of oversharpening. It's always a good idea to work on a duplicate of the background layer. If the sharpening effect is too strong, you can lower the layer's opacity to reduce the effect.

Figure 9-3. *A comparison of the original image, the image sharpened using the default settings, and the image oversharpened*

Tutorial 34: Sharpening Using the Unsharp Mask Filter

In this tutorial, you'll use the Unsharp Mask filter to sharpen the image of the coat of arms on the castle wall.

To sharpen this image, follow these steps:

1. Open the picture of the castle wall (*Ch9_coat-of-arms*) found in the Practice Images folder. Duplicate the background layer and rename it *Sharpen* (Figure 9-4).

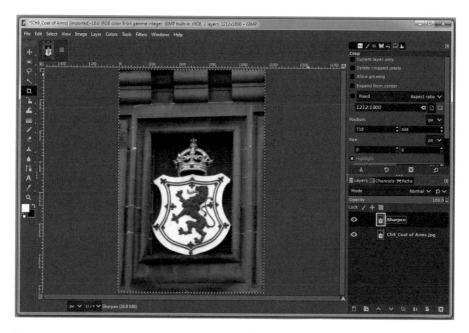

Figure 9-4. *A duplicate layer created to use the Unsharp Mask filter on*

2. Open the Unsharp Mask dialog (Filters ➤ Enhance ➤ Unsharp Mask).

3. Set the Radius to 1.5, leaving the others at their default settings (Figure 9-5).

Figure 9-5. *Using the Unsharp Mask dialog*

I zoomed in on the crown in this before and after comparison, showing a subtle increase in sharpness (Figure 9-6).

Figure 9-6. *The before and after comparison*

High Pass Sharpening

The High Pass method sharpens an image's edges without affecting the area between them. This is generally considered a better way to sharpen images than Unsharp Mask, at least in certain instances.

Tutorial 35: Sharpening Using the High Pass Filter

In this tutorial, you'll sharpen the image of the baby using the High Pass technique. The G'MIC plug-in must be installed for this lesson.

To sharpen this image, follow these steps:

1. Open the picture of the baby (*Ch9_baby*) found in the Practice Images folder. Duplicate the background layer and rename it *Sharpen* (Figure 9-7).

Figure 9-7. *A duplicate layer created to use the High Pass sharpen technique on*

2. Apply the High Pass filter (Image Menu ➤ Filters ➤ G'MIC).

3. Click the triangle (or + sign) next to Details to open the available options and select High Pass. Adjust the Radius to 4.00 and leave the Contrast setting at 2.00 (Figure 9-8).

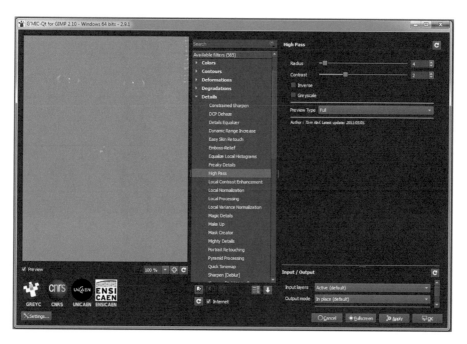

Figure 9-8. *Applying the High Pass filter*

4. The High Pass filter emphasizes the edges of the
    image (Figure 9-9).

Figure 9-9. *The High Pass filter emphasizes the edges of the image*

5. Change the blend mode of the Sharpen layer to
    Overlay (Figure 9-10). This will slightly boost the
    contrast of the edges, improving the appearance of
    sharpness without accentuating the film grain.

Figure 9-10. *The appearance of sharpness is enhanced*

The High Pass method of sharpening is generally very effective yet gentle, so the destructive effects are kept to a minimum. Although the difference is subtle, the image has more snap compared to the original (Figure 9-11).

Figure 9-11. *The before and after comparison*

Another way of sharpening images in GIMP is called "smart" sharpening, which in essence sharpens the edges of an image without accentuating the grain or noise. The technique is in the GIMP tutorials found on the official website here: `www.gimp.org/tutorials/Smart_Sharpening/`.

Summary

Images can often benefit from a light application of the Unsharp Mask filter; however, it can accentuate film grain and digital noise and, when overused, create unwanted artifacts around edges. For a gentler type of sharpening, the High Pass method enhances the edges of the image without overaccentuating film grain or digital noise. We also learned that GIMP is capable of "smart" sharpening, a technique that allows one to sharpen the edges of an image without overaccentuating grain or noise; the technique can be found in the GIMP tutorial here: `www.gimp.org/tutorials/Smart_Sharpening/`.

CHAPTER 10

Fun and Artistic Projects with Your Photos

In This Chapter

- Turn Photos into Digital Works of Art
- Creating Collages

Turn Photos into Digital Works of Art

GIMP offers a number of filters that can turn your images into digital works of art. Image retouching and restoration can be tedious and difficult work at times, so this can be a fun way to work with your images. You can experiment to your heart's content without the messiness of actual paints, brushes, or inks.

© Phillip Whitt 2023
P. Whitt, *Beginning Photo Retouching and Restoration Using GIMP*,
https://doi.org/10.1007/978-1-4842-9265-5_10

For the professional retoucher, converting photographs into digital art can be an added service to offer to clients. For the hobbyist, it can be a fun and creative way to make gifts for family and friends or even spruce up decor.

Figure 10-1 illustrates two different artistic filters applied to the photograph of the Mill Mountain Star: Photocopy (center) and Predator (bottom).

Figure 10-1. *Examples of the Photocopy (center) and Predator (bottom) artistic filters*

The artistic filters are nested in GIMP's Filters (Image Menu ➤ Filters ➤ Artistic). You can control various parameters of the filter. For example, when converting an image to a digital oil painting using the Oilify filter, you can control how detailed it appears. Increasing the mask gives it more of a "painterly" look (Figure 10-2).

Figure 10-2. *Applying the Oilify filter to create the appearance of a painting*

After applying the Oilify filter, this image was finished by using the Apply Canvas filter. The result is a facsimile of an oil painting (Figure 10-3).

Figure 10-3. *A digital facsimile of an oil painting*

Add Artistic Functionality with G'MIC

The G'MIC plug-in offers a ton of options for adding artistic effects. It's well worth taking the time to become familiar with it, to bring out your "inner artist," especially if traditional art materials aren't your strong suit. G'MIC is available from https://gmic.eu/.

The image in Figure 10-4 was converted into a digital pen-and-ink style drawing, by using the Pen Drawing filter nested within the G'MIC filters.

Figure 10-4. *An example of the Pen Drawing filter included in the G'MIC plug-in*

Art Project No. 1: Salvaging "Unfixable" Photos

Some of your photos may have focus issues that can't be repaired in the conventional sense of image editing. The example in Figure 10-5 is one of many photographs I shot in New Orleans in 1993. Most of them turned out fine, but as you can imagine, I was very disappointed at how out of focus this one turned out.

Figure 10-5. *A blurry photograph that has potential to become digital art*

It won't be possible to get a good photograph from this image. Even the Unsharp Mask filter can't make much of an improvement; there's just no sharp detail to rescue. Although it's not a usable image as a photograph, it does have potential as digital art. If you'd like to give this technique a try, this image (Ch10_blurry_girl) is located in the Practice Images folder. Then try it on some of your own images. Of course, this technique doesn't have to be limited to out-of-focus images. Use it on any of your favorite pictures that would look great as digital art.

You must have the G'MIC plug-in installed for this exercise.

1. Open the image (*Ch10_blurry_girl*) and apply the Rodilius filter (Image Menu ➤ Filters ➤ G'MIC-Qt).

2. With the G'MIC dialog box open, click the small triangle (or + sign on Windows) next to the Artistic option (Figure 10-6).

Figure 10-6. *The Artistic option in the G'MIC dialog box*

3.   Select the Rodilius filter. I dialed the Amplitude
      setting back to 7.00 but left the other options at their
      default settings (Figure 10-7).

Figure 10-7. *Applying the Rodilius filter*

The end result is an image that is quite usable as digital art. Of course, my preference would be a photograph that is sharp and in focus. Because that isn't possible, I was able to preserve the essence of the original image that (I think) many would find an acceptable and pleasing alternative (Figure 10-8).

Figure 10-8. *The resulting digital art from a blurry photograph*

After trying this on your own photographs, experiment with different filters. Because art is subjective, you might not like the results from using the Rodilius filter and would prefer a different style. If you have similar photos that can't be saved by conventional restoration, this might be the ticket to salvage those less-than-perfect images. If you like the results, you can enlarge the image and have it framed or printed on canvas at your local photo lab or by an online service (Figure 10-9).

Figure 10-9. *Newly created digital art can be framed or printed on canvas*

Creating Collages

With some imagination, you can assemble your photos into themed collages. A collage can be the perfect gift for sentimental family members (or family members that are hard to find gifts for). Collages don't necessarily have to be themed. They can be composed of your favorite family photographs. The example in Figure 10-10 was well received by my now deceased father-in-law as a Christmas present. The images in the collage span the time from his wedding day to his 80th birthday.

Figure 10-10. *A collage of family photos spanning time*

Art Project No. 2: Assembling a Collage

If you've never created a collage before and would like to re-create this one for practice (Figure 10-11), you'll find all of the images contained in the Scottish Collage folder located in the Practice Images folder.

Figure 10-11. *A collage of images taken in Scotland in 2012*

1. Open the Brick Walkway image (*Ch10_Brick_ Background*).

2. Open the Hue/Saturation dialog (Image Menu ➤ Colors ➤ Hue-Saturation). Set the Lightness value to 75 to give it a subtle, washed-out appearance (Figure 10-12).

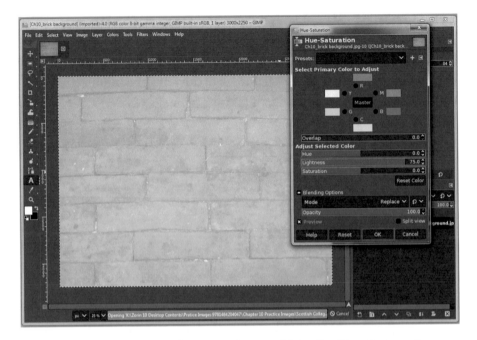

Figure 10-12. *Set the Lightness value to 75 in the Hue-Saturation dialog box*

3. Open each image and use the Rectangle Select tool (R). Set the Feather Edges option to a radius of 50 pixels.

4. Make a selection around the image, allowing adequate space within the image edge (Figure 10-13). Copy the selection to the clipboard (Control + C).

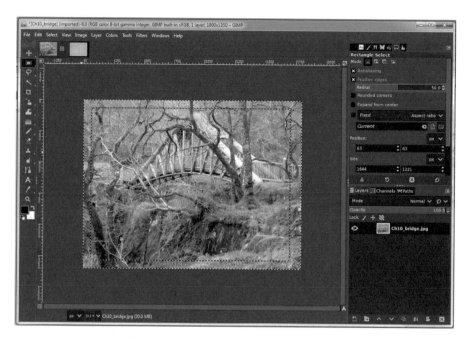

Figure 10-13. *Making a selection within the image edge*

5. Paste it as a new layer (Image Menu ➤ Edit ➤
    Paste As ➤ New Layer) into the collage in progress
    (Figure 10-14). Scale and arrange the layer orders as
    necessary to use the background layer as a border.

Figure 10-14. *Pasting as a new layer to the collage in progress*

6. Open the Text tool (T) and, using the URW Chancery
    L Medium font (or another similar font), set at 200
    pixels and type "Scotland 2012".

Don't worry if your results don't exactly match the example. The idea is
to get a feel for the process. If you get to a point where you make collages on
a regular basis, you'll likely develop your own style. You can also visit online
services that offer predesigned templates for collages. One such service is
PicMonkey (`www.picmonkey.com/`). Log on to see the options offered.

Summary

GIMP is not only useful for image retouching and restoration, it also offers
many filters for creating works of art from photos. The G'MIC plug-in
expands the options of artistic filters, offering literally hundreds to choose
from. You can give photographs that are out of focus and can't otherwise

314

be repaired new life as works of art, by utilizing one of the many filters that capture the essence of the image—the next best thing to actually repairing it. Any of your favorite photographs are good candidates for conversion to digital art.

Assembling collages is a fun way to display your images. You can create themed collages to commemorate special events, or a collage can be a collection of your favorite photos from past to present. Collages make great gifts for sentimental family members, and most will appreciate them.

CHAPTER 11

Printing and Preserving Your Images

In This Chapter

- Photo-Quality Printers
- Protecting and Preserving Your Prints
- Storing Images Digitally

Photo-Quality Printers

Photo-quality printers have come a long way from the first-generation models that were around in the early 1990s. The output quality rivals that of traditional photo lab prints. The prints produced from those early models (particularly ink-jet printers) were prone to rapid fading—sometimes in a matter of months. Obviously, you want your prints to be the best quality available, as well as to last for generations. This is especially important when providing your services to paying customers.

© Phillip Whitt 2023
P. Whitt, *Beginning Photo Retouching and Restoration Using GIMP*,
https://doi.org/10.1007/978-1-4842-9265-5_11

Ink-Jet Printers

Photo-quality ink-jet printers have advanced by leaps and bounds over the years. The papers and inks used by modern printers are capable of producing beautiful, high-resolution images (Figure 11-1). Ink-jet printers spray on paper micro-sized dots that make up the image. The dots are only visible when the image is greatly magnified, not when viewing a print with the unaided eye.

Figure 11-1. *Modern ink-jet printers can produce high-quality images. (Image courtesy of George Milton/Pexels)*

Ink-jet printers are designed to use one of two types of ink: dye based or pigment based. Most models use dye-based inks, but there are some high-end models geared toward the professional that use pigment-based inks to produce archival-quality prints that are rated to last about 200 years when framed under glass and displayed under normal lighting conditions. Even some models using dye-based inks (when combined with the paper it's formulated for) will produce prints that are rated to last for about 75–100 years under the same conditions.

Desktop photo-quality ink-jet printers are available in small models that print 4" × 6" images to large-format models that produce prints up to 13" × 19". While general-purpose ink-jet printers use four ink colors (CMYK), dedicated photo-quality printers use (depending on the manufacturer) colors such as red, orange, green, and variations of black. This offers the widest color gamut possible. There are a variety of photo-quality ink-jet papers available, such as gloss, semigloss, and matte (flat). Most photo-quality printers are designed to use their own brand of inks and paper, for the best results and maximum life span.

One of the main disadvantages of ink-jet prints is that they are generally not very water-resistant, so they must be kept dry. Even a single drop can ruin a print.

Dye-Sublimation Printers

Dye-sublimation (also known as dye-sub) printers have been around for a while and are commonly used in digital photo labs. They work by using a thermal process to transfer dye contained on a ribbon to the surface of the paper. Dye-sublimation printers produce very high-quality prints that are continuous in tone and more water-resistant than ink-jet prints. One disadvantage of dye-sublimation printers is that they are usually limited to glossy paper and only print up to 8" × 10" (with the exception of some wide-format commercial models costing thousands of dollars). Another is that the paper and ink ribbons they require are expensive, compared to their ink-jet counterparts.

Dye-sublimation printers have made their way into the consumer market in recent years and are well worth looking at while conducting your research, if you are considering which type of printer to buy. Either type will produce high-quality prints—which type to choose will depend on your particular needs (and print longevity should be considered as well).

Tip   Log on to the Wilhelm Imaging Research website (`www.wilhelm-research.com`) for data concerning the longevity performance of various printer and paper manufacturers.

Protecting and Preserving Your Prints

After you've gone through the hard work of editing your image (or possibly many images), you will probably be highly motivated to protect your newly printed pictures (as well as your original photographic materials) from potential harm. Many of the images you restored may have been damaged, because they were kept in catchall boxes, drawers, or other places where miscellaneous household objects are stored. Others may have faded, because they were displayed in frames and exposed to UV light over the years. Proper archiving will avoid those mishaps from occurring again.

Archiving Your Prints

There are many products available to archive your prints (as well as negatives and slides): acid-free sleeves for three-ring binders (Figure 11-2), storage boxes, and albums are some examples. These products can be purchased at your local camera shop or an online supplier such as B&H Photo (`www.bhphotovideo.com`).

Figure 11-2. *Photo archival sleeve for use in a three-ring binder*

Cheap photo albums with "magnetic" pages should be avoided; they use a thin layer of tacky adhesive to secure the photograph on the album page. The materials used in the album may damage the photos over time. In Figure 11-3, you can see a page that is deteriorating in an album purchased in the early 1990s. There is also a risk the photos will eventually be permanently stuck to the page.

Figure 11-3. *Cheap photo albums can potentially damage your prints over time*

After archiving your photographic materials, make sure they are stored in a cool, dark place with low humidity. Avoid keeping them in places with temperature extremes, such as attics and garages, as these are prime breeding grounds for mold and fungus.

It's a good idea to make sure that all of your photographic materials are digitized as well as archived. It can be a big job if your prints, negatives, and slides number in the hundreds or thousands, but it's well worth the time and effort to preserve your family history. It can be a long-term project; it doesn't have to be done all at once.

Displaying Your Prints

For the new prints you want to display, a good-quality frame using acid-free materials is important. Like cheap photo albums, poor-quality materials in frames can be destructive. The ink-jet print image in Figure 11-4 began to discolor along the bottom in a few short years, because the mat the print came in contact with was of poor quality.

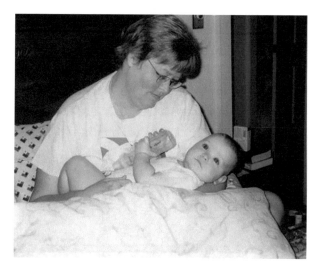

Figure 11-4. *Cheap materials in a frame caused discoloration in this ink-jet print*

It's obvious that for important prints, cheap frames from the discount store should be avoided. Your local custom frame shop can provide frames that use high-quality materials. Many have UV-resistant glass that will help extend print longevity.

For an added layer of protection, special spray lacquers formulated for ink-jet prints are available that protect the image from UV light, dirt, moisture, and other contaminants. They are available in gloss, satin, and matte, to match the type of paper your pictures are printed on.

If you use a spray lacquer, read the directions carefully and follow all of the safety instructions. Use in well-ventilated areas and keep away from open flames.

Storing Images Digitally

It's important to exercise the same care in the storage of your digital images that you would extend to the printed versions. They serve the same purpose as negatives do in relation to traditional photographs; they are backup copies. The images currently on your computer should be backed up as soon as possible, either to an external hard drive (Figure 11-5), flash drive, SD card, or disk, such as a CD-ROM or DVD. For maximum protection, consider using multiple types of media.

Figure 11-5. *Backing up images to an external hard drive is one way to help preserve them. (Image courtesy of George Milton/Pexels)*

It's a good idea to keep your digitally archived images stored in multiple locations. You can keep extra copies on a CD-ROM, DVD, flash drive, or external hard drive in a safe-deposit box or with a trusted family member. If the unthinkable, such as a fire, flood, or other disasters, occurs, at least you'll have copies of your treasured memories preserved.

There is also the option of online data storage services (commonly referred to as the "cloud"). These services have become popular in the past several years. There are a couple of noteworthy benefits, such as the ability to share your photos anytime and anywhere you have Internet access. Also, they routinely back up their data, so the risk of loss is small. However, I personally wouldn't feel entirely comfortable storing my images on a cloud service exclusively. If you choose to use the cloud, I recommend using *at least* one other method of storing your images.

Follow the same guidelines for storing electronic media as you would photographic materials—protect your external hard drives, flash drives, and disks from temperature extremes and high humidity. Keep disks safe and organized in archival sleeves or storage boxes.

How Long Will Digital Images Last?

It would seem logical to assume that digital images will last forever, but it's not necessarily that simple. The digital storage devices of today might very well be obsolete in the not too distant future. Optical disks, such as the CD-ROM and DVD, could suffer the same fate as VHS tapes. Even if there are devices that can read them 20, 30, or 40 years from now, the data might become corrupted over time.

It will likely be a matter of migrating your images to the most current storage devices every few years. If you have images stored on an older external hard drive, you might consider transferring them to one of the newer, solid-state models (the data should be accessed about every six months, to avoid potential loss). Images that are stored on old CDs (from the late 1990s or early 2000s) should be transferred to newer disks. (There are archival-quality disks available that are estimated to last up to 300 years.)

If you have images stored in an online cloud service, what would happen if the company went out of business? Or if your photos were accidentally deleted? I wouldn't bet that it couldn't happen (it probably already has). The expression "Don't put all your eggs in one basket" comes to mind.

Video Montages

One added benefit of digitizing your images is they can be assembled into a video montage, using slide show software. In addition to paid programs, there are a number of free titles available that allow you to add transitions and music. Figure 11-6 is an example of a free program for Debian-based Linux distributions called *PhotoFilmStrip*. (There are also free programs for Windows and Mac systems.) It's more convenient than flipping through a photo album. The production can be put onto a disk, such as a DVD, or uploaded to mobile devices. For the professional retoucher, this can be a great add-on service to provide. Customers will often purchase multiple copies on disk to give as gifts.

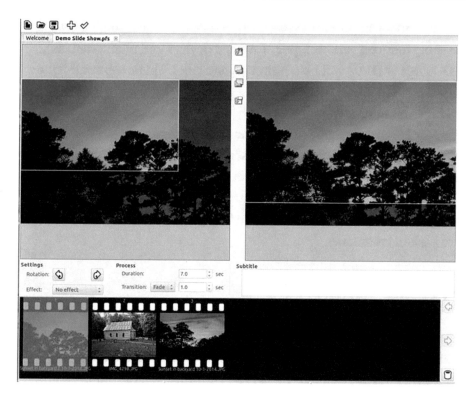

Figure 11-6. PhotoFilmStrip is a free slide show program for Debian-based Linux distributions

Summary

In this chapter, I covered the attributes of photo-quality printers, as well as the expected longevity of images printed using archival paper and ink. Storing and displaying prints properly is important for long-term preservation. Environments having high humidity and temperature extremes should be avoided. Cheap photo albums and picture frames can potentially damage your images. Storage sleeves, boxes, albums, and frames should be made of high-quality, acid-free materials.

It's equally important to exercise great care in storing digital images. Keeping them on various types of storage devices and media such as CD-ROMs or DVDs will help protect against loss. This is especially true when copies are kept "off-site," such as in a safe-deposit box, with a trusted relative, or online storage service.

Migrating your digital images to current storage devices every few years can help "future-proof" them should the current technology become obsolete and unavailable to access your images years from now.

Using software to create video montages is a great way to share images with family members and can be a great add-on service for the professional retoucher.

Closing Thoughts

I hope you've enjoyed working on the tutorials and that you learned a lot from this book. You can take what you've learned and apply it to your own images. Each new image you edit will probably require some experimentation, but the techniques outlined in this publication should take a great deal of the trial and error out of the process.

Just remember to keep learning and keep practicing!

Index

A

Acid-free materials, 323

Active color, 156, 168, 249, 259, 261, 267

Additive color, 101

Airbrush tool, 249, 250

Amount, 289

Artistic filters, 300, 302, 314

Artistic functionality, 303, 304

Artistic option, 305, 306

Auto Input Levels, 107–114

Auto-settings, 47–49

Auto-sharping feature, 287

B

Background color, 226, 227

Background layer, 25, 28, 39, 44, 67, 73, 77, 82, 87, 95, 108, 114, 119, 123, 138, 177, 184, 192, 241, 249, 260, 262, 263, 265, 266, 271, 273, 276

Backgrounds replacing, 257–275

BitTorrent, 5, 7

Black-and-white
colorizing, 165–172
conversions, 149
image, 154
portrait, 141
sitcom, 154

Black point slider, 123, 124, 201, 213

Blemishes, 183

Blending modes, 28, 71, 85

Blend mode, 88, 179

Blue channel, 125, 133, 149, 191

Brick Walkway image, 311

Brightest range, 59

Brightness-Contrast dialog, 75–78

Brush tools, 18–21

Burn tool, 126, 136, 272

C

Camera, 35–38

Canvas filter, 302

Channels, 104–106, 191, 195

Clean-up work, 181, 193, 196

Clone tool, 19, 181, 182, 187, 188, 192, 193, 196, 198, 199, 206, 208, 211, 215, 216, 218, 231, 242, 281, 283, 284

Cloning, 25, 206, 207, 244, 286

Cloud service, 325, 326

© Phillip Whitt 2023
P. Whitt, *Beginning Photo Retouching and Restoration Using GIMP*,
https://doi.org/10.1007/978-1-4842-9265-5

W, X, Y

Z

Printed in the United States
by Baker & Taylor Publisher Services